*It's Awesome, Baby –
with a capital A!*

*– Dickie V*

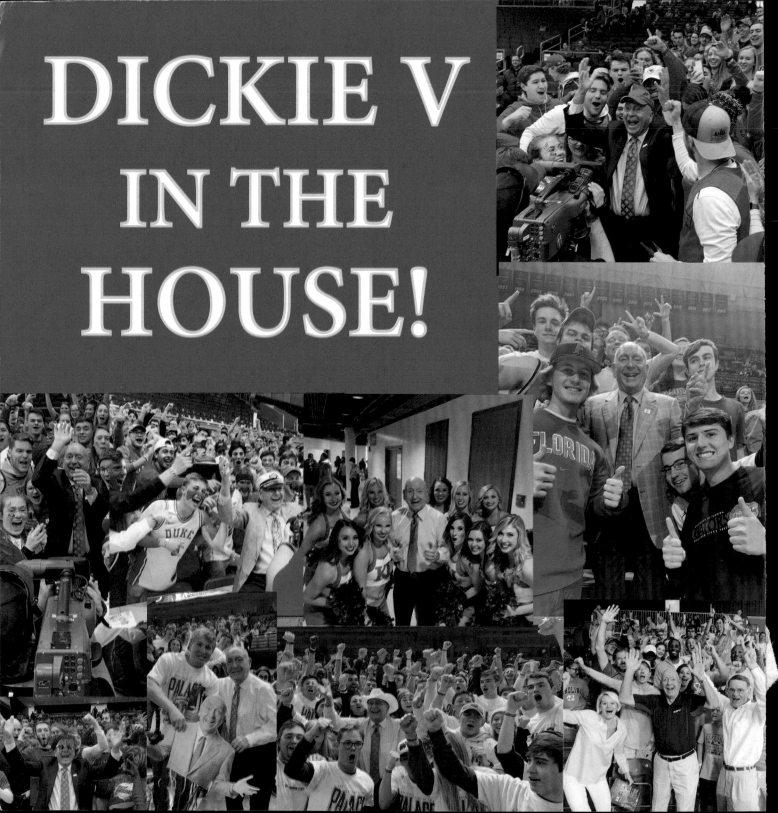

# DICKIE V
# IN THE
# HOUSE!

ISBN: 978-1945907586

Published by Nico 11 Publishing & Design | Mukwonago, Wisconsin
Publisher: Michael Nicloy
Quantity order requests may be emailed to: mike@nico11publishing.com

***The Lost Season***
***A look at what the journey to the 2020 National Championship could have been***

Author: Dick Vitale
Contributing Author: Dick Weiss
Research and Contributing Editor: Howie Schwab
Foreword: Leonard Hamilton
Associate Editors: Reji Laberje, Griffin Mill
Proofreader: Lyda Rose Haerle
Interior and Cover Layout: Michael Nicloy
Cover Design: Michael Nicloy, Sara Sauer
Front cover image (Dick Vitale Headshot): Phil Ellsworth/ESPN Images
Cover Bracket: Griffin Mill

"DICKIE V IN THE HOUSE!" photo collage:
Layout: Michael Nicloy
Images courtesy of Dick Vitale

Every reasonable attempt has been made to determine the ownership of copyright and proper credit of images used in this book.

Printed in The United States of America

# THE LOST SEASON

*A look at what the journey to the*
*2020 National Championship could have been*

# DICK VITALE

## with Dick Weiss

## Research by Howie Schwab

## Foreword by Leonard Hamilton

ISBN: 978-1945907586

Published by Nico 11 Publishing & Design
www.nico11publishing.com

Be well read.

I want to dedicate this book to all of these beautiful young kids who have or their families have been to my gala over the years. They will be missed, but certainly not forgotten.

- Dick Vitale

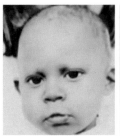

**ADRIAN LITTLEJOHN**
FEBRUARY 4, 2010-
MAY 1, 2011

**LACEY HOLSWORTH**
NOVEMBER 30, 2005-
APRIL 8, 2014

**PAYTON WRIGHT**
MAY 7, 2002-
MAY 29, 2007

**CHAD CARR**
SEPTEMBER 26, 2010-
NOVEMBER 23, 2015

**EDDIE LIVINGSTON**
SEPTEMBER 3, 2006-
NOVEMBER 24, 2013

**DILLON SIMMONS**
NOVEMBER 2, 1998-
APRIL, 25, 2014

**LUCY WEBER**
JUNE 8, 2009-
NOVEMBER 20, 2010

**JUSTIN MILLER**
APRIL 21, 1992-
APRIL 3, 2013

**CALEB JACOBBE**
FEBRUARY 4, 1998-
MAY 10, 2006

**DAVID HEARD**
MAY 5, 2000-
FEBRUARY 10, 2011

**JOHNNY TEIS**
AUGUST 1, 2002-
APRIL 11, 2011

**JULIA MOUNTS**
OCTOBER 8, 2002-
APRIL 23, 2016

**AUSTIN SCHROEDER**
AUGUST 13, 1999-
APRIL 28, 2015

**LAUREN HILL**
OCTOBER 1, 1995-
APRIL 10, 2015

**LUKE KELLY**
JANUARY 27, 2010-
JANUARY 19, 2015

**BENJAMIN GILKEY**
DECEMBER 22, 2007-
FEBRUARY 11, 2017

**TONER (TONY) COLTON**
OCTOBER 18, 1999-
JULY 30, 2017

**CLAYTON MATHEW VAN LANDUYT**
OCTOBER 19, 2015-
AUGUST 20, 2019

To my wife Joan, an English major who loves books and has been totally supportive every step of the way through this pandemic, and to all the people at the V Foundation who work tirelessly to make life better for children with pediatric cancer.

- Dick Weiss


To my wife Suzie, who inspires me every day. I want to thank my mom (Dona), my dad (Ted), my sister (Elysa) and brother-in-law (Bobby) for their support always. I appreciate my closest friends, Bob Pollicino, Barry Sacks, Joe McEnerney, Ross Arnel, and Mike Vettor for their phone calls of encouragement throughout the season.

- Howie Schwab

# THE LOST SEASON

# TABLE OF CONTENTS

# TABLE OF CONTENTS

# /ORD

## Hamilton

...new we had a chance to be a good basketball team. ...9 by winning 12 of our last 13 games, advancing to ...rning a No. 3 seed in the NCAA Tournament. We

the A(
were

T
Febr
seni
and
seco
tale
seas

the
rett
in
ou
ho

wi
an

...us in
...of our
...re hurt
...for the
...st to a
...ng our

...enced by
...ueled the
...verybody
...ay during
...rated just

...finished
...l victories

*Photo credit: Ross Obley*

*Leonard Hamilton led Florida State to
its first ACC regular season title.*

Even though we had to replace six players who all played major roles in our success, my staff and I felt good about the group of players we had returning for the 2020 season. They had all played significant minutes in big games against great teams in arenas full of fans…who are not kind to their opponents.

The instinctive ability of our coaching staff to communicate with our players was a key to our success. Stan Jones, Charlton (CY) Young, Mike Bradley, and the great addition of Steve Smith to our staff continues to make our staff one of the best in the nation.

At Florida State, we have developed a system. And we are who we are because our players believe in our system, our culture, and our offensive and defensive systems. All of the players are going to have the chance to help us win games. The system that is successful for us allows our team to win by committee. Every player in our program knows his role and that, in any game, it could be his time to shine.

We believed we had the talent, depth, and defensive ability to be a really good team in March.

Florida State guard Trent Forrest averaged 11.6 ppg. and four apg. during the 2019-20 season.

Returnees Trent Forrest, M.J. Walker, and Devin Vassell led the way. Their continued development was important. Forrest is such an unselfish player; he does everything well and doesn't always get the recognition he deserves. RaiQuan Gray, Anthony Polite, and Wyatt Wilkes were going to have expanded roles as returning players who were comfortable with our system, and newcomers Patrick Williams, Dominik Olejniczak, Balsa Koprivica, and RayQuan Evans were going to have to learn quickly as we had put together one of the tougher schedules in the country. The unbelievable attitude and progress made by our newcomers was a key factor in our success. And, for the first time, we would play 20 ACC games against some of the most tradition-rich programs in the nation, in the best college basketball conference ever assembled.

We had the right ingredients of experience and talent to play at a high level. The chemistry our guys developed between themselves and our staff is what set our team apart and is a difference-maker in building a successful program.

Along the way, we grew even closer, winning a number of hard-fought, close games. We were unbeaten at home—the only ACC team able to make that claim—and our fans at the Tucker Center were phenomenal. There were road wins at Florida, Louisville, and

Notre Dame, where we prevailed in the last second. Whether coming from behind or leading from the start, we found ways to win, finishing with a 26-5 record, including a program-best 16-4 ACC record.

We are 65-3 at home in the last five years and have made our home court one of the toughest places to play in the country.

We won the ACC regular season championship with a victory over Boston College in what turned out to be our final game of the season. I wanted our players and staff to know the feeling of cutting down nets and celebrating with each other, so we did just that. The joy felt by my players as they celebrated with their families, their friends, and everyone who supported us is a feeling none of us are ever going to forget.

I woke up with an uneasy feeling on the morning of our first game in the ACC Tournament. My fears were realized shortly before tip-off against Clemson, when we learned the tournament had been canceled as a result of the coronavirus pandemic.

My team was disappointed to not be competing for a championship, but also understood why things played out the way that they did. We were all bitterly disappointed when the full NCAA Tournament was canceled a short time later.

*As a coach, you always work to prepare for every situation. This was a circumstance none of us could have anticipated; one that will be chronicled in history books.*

We will all be stronger for what we encountered through our remarkable 2019-2020 journey together and we will persevere as we move forward.

Our tradition, our culture, and our belief in our system has us positioned for continued success. We are one of the top four winningest programs in the ACC in the last 15 years, and our mindset is to continue moving into the upper echelon of college basketball.

As Florida State competes successfully amongst the world of Blue Bloods in college basketball, we consider ourselves to be the New Bloods.

*Photo credit: Mitch White*

# INTRODUCTION

The end of the 2020 NCAA men's basketball season was supposed to take place April 6 in Atlanta, Georgia. Over 80,000 fans were expected to attend the NCAA's annual Final Four at Mercedes-Benz Stadium.

Unfortunately, the massive outbreak of the global coronavirus pandemic put a sudden end to the men's and women's tournaments almost a month earlier than expected. The shutdown occurred on March 12th, the same day the Power Conference tournaments were canceled, two hours after a frantic meeting.

The unprecedented move came a day after the NCAA announced the games that were scheduled to start the following week would go on but would be played in mostly empty arenas. That plan was scrapped as every major American sports league from the NBA to Major League Baseball turned off the keys over concerns about the pandemic, and all the NCAA's winter and spring championships were shut down.

The NCAA had no other choice but to cancel March Madness. Once conferences began cancelling their league tournaments, the optics of the NCAA holding a national tournament and putting unpaid student-athletes at serious medical risk, all in order to make money off TV, looked worse than ever.

No game is more important than the health and safety of everyone involved, and this was one time when sports had to take a back seat to the concerns of public health.

My heart goes out to all the players, coachesc and fans who dreamed about being part of this magical three-week experience. I believe March Madness is the greatest sporting event in America.

So, let's take a moment and salute seniors like Markus Howard of Marquette, Myles Powell of Seton Hall, Payton Pritchard of Oregon, and Cassius Winston of Michigan State, who played their last collegiate games.

*Marquette Athletics*

*Markus Howard completed his career as Marquette's all-time leading scorer.*

Luka Garza of Iowa was a junior and Obi Toppin of Dayton was a sophomore. Garza and Toppin entered the NBA Draft, though Garza could still pull out.

So many coaches believed they had a legitimate shot to cut down the nets in this wild college basketball season.

The 2019-2020 season would have included a number of interesting storylines. Yale coach James Jones and his brother, Joe, from Boston University would have been in the field together; Rutgers getting in for the first time since 1991; Liberty from the Atlantic Sun and East Tennessee State from the Southern Conference, both 30-game winners, already punched their tickets. I have often said, March Madness is one of the greatest sporting events. This year, it was sent to the sidelines.

The day after the NCAA announced the cancellation of the tournament, I went on ESPN's "SportsCenter" and "Get Up" and asked why the NCAA couldn't have postponed it with a rescheduled event, perhaps with fewer teams, down the line. I thought, initially, a pause would have been better, following the pattern of what Adam Silver and the NBA were doing. The NCAA doesn't have anyone like that, a liaison between the NCAA and the college game. College basketball needs a czar. I thought it was embarrassing that the college tournaments were being played and there was no decision on the NCAA tournament. So, I went the route of saying initially they should not have postponed it.

I need to give Mark Emmert and his people credit for this decision. They reached out to the people in infectious diseases and they came back with this: No way, shape, or form are you going to be playing basketball in April or May. If you go beyond that, teams just can't come out and play. You've got to practice. You've got the NBA draft. You've got players graduating.

The health and safety of our people takes priority.

Nobody loves the game any more than I do.

Nobody loves the tournament any more than I do.

It's the greatest sporting event in America. For three weeks, March Madness captivates the hearts of the American sports fans. Grandma, Grandpa, everybody gets involved. They put sweatshirts on, cheering, screaming, and yelling for their teams.

It's heartbreaking for the seniors, but the end result is this: If that's the biggest disappointment those kids will have in their life, they will have had one heck of a life. But the bottom line: basketball had to go to the bench. Our biggest priority is defeating coronavirus and getting it under control.

I came up with the idea of this book to get some feelings off my chest. It's almost like therapy. What could have been, should have been, and would have been. And this book is going to be a special journey in terms of the chase for the national championship. We can all sit and think we're all experts and really project what's going to happen.

Even when you're Kansas, Gonzaga, the teams on top. Every team is beatable. I tell you that those second-round games would have been magical. Kansas and Gonzaga playing against those 8-9 guys. I don't think there is much difference on a neutral court with the three-point shot. I think more teams than in any other year—and I've been doing games for 41 years—could have legitimately won the national championship. So much for the event, until I went to the VBDI (Vitale Bald Dome Index). I know this is speculative, but what if the field of 68 had been announced and the tournament had been held?

*Cassius Winston finished his career as the Big Ten assist leader.*

Selection Sunday is one of my favorite days of the year. Cinderellas are seeded. Surprise teams earn invites to the big dance.

Let's have some fun.

I understand some fans will be disappointed with my opinions, but we didn't have the games played, so this will have to do.

I hope college hoop fans enjoy this.

All of my proceeds from the sale of this book will be donated to The V Foundation for Pediatric Cancer Research. Please donate at www.dickvitale.com.

# CHAPTER ONE

---

# KANSAS COMES IN NUMBER ONE

Kansas was everybody's No. 1 before March Madness started.

The regular season Big 12 champions were 28-3 when the season abruptly ended after the first day of the conference tournament March 11. The Jayhawks were a near-unanimous No. 1 in the final regular season AP Top 25 and the Coaches Poll, receiving 63 of 65 first place votes from the national media panel, and 29 of 32 from the coaches' group. It was the fourth time the Jayhawks had finished first in the poll, which was established in 1947.

The Jayhawks were also one of the teams that lost the most when the NCAA Tournament was canceled. They were a lock for a No. 1 regional seed, no matter what happened in the Big 12 tournament.

I was fortunate enough to call several Kansas games during the season. The last was a huge 66-62 victory over Texas Tech in an electric atmosphere at Lubbock against the defending national runner up, which had lost three straight and was hungry for a W. Kansas knew they were going to get Texas Tech's best shot. It was a real battle in which 7'0", 267-pound senior center Udoka Azubuike had 15 points and 11 rebounds as Kansas clinched its 19th Big 12 title outright in the 24-year history of the league with a 17-1 record.

At the end of the year, Bill Self just started pounding the ball inside to Azubuike, who was just a nightmare for many teams that didn't have someone to play him.

"That's the best Kansas team I've seen," Texas Tech coach Chris Beard said. "Dev Dotson (is) the best guard in college basketball, Dok's the best big in college basketball, and Myles Garrett is the best defender in college basketball, and their role players don't make mistakes."

Self's team was one of the favorites to cut down the nets in Atlanta. The Jayhawks won more games than anyone in Big 12 conference history.

Rock, chalk, Jayhawk was on fire, winning their final 16 games of the season, which tied for the fifth-longest streak of the Self era, which began in 2003-2004.

The Jayhawks had one of the top trios in America in Dotson, Azubuike and Garrett. Azubuike and Dotson were both second team AP All-Americans. Azubuike was the 2019-2020 Big 12 Player of the Year, first team All-Big 12 and a finalist for the Kareem Abdul-Jabbar Center of the Year award. The senior, who came to the United States from Nigeria in 2014 to get an education, passed on the NBA draft to return to Lawrence.

*Devon Dotson led the Big 12 in scoring at 18.1 ppg.*

His presence was even bigger than his frame. Azubuike led the NCAA in field goal percentage at 74.8. He is now the NCAA career field goal percentage leader at 74.4 percent, surpassing Tacko Fall of UCF at 74.0 in 2019. He also led the Big 12 in rebounding with 10.5 per game and led the Big 12 in double-doubles with 15. Azubuike was second in the Big 12 in blocked shots per game at 2.6.

Dotson, a sophomore guard who toyed with the idea of turning pro the previous year, led the Big 12 in several categories—scoring at 18.1 points, 2.1 steals, and 142 free throws made. He also ranked among the Big 12 leaders in 20-point games (second at nine), field goal percentage (second at 46.8), free throw percentage (fifth at 83.0), assists (fifth at 4.0), and assist-to-turnover ratio (fifth at 1.7). Dotson became just the fifth Jayhawk to lead the Big 12 in scoring, joining Drew Gooden in 2002, Wayne Simien in 2005, Frank Mason III in 2017, and Dedric Lawson in 2019.

Garrett led the Big 12 in assists (4.6) and assist-to-turnover ratio (2.7). He was also ranked among the Big 12 leaders in steals (fifth at 1.8). The Big 12 Defensive Player of the Year, he was also the Naismith Defensive Player of the Year.

*Udoka Azubuike led the nation in field goal percentage at 74.8 pct.*

Kansas started the season with a tough 68-66 loss to Duke in the Champions Classic at Madison Square Garden. The Jayhawks won 28 of their next 30 games, with their only other losses coming at Villanova and against Baylor.

There were a couple hiccups along the way. Entering the season, the program and Self were hit with an NCAA notice of allegations stemming from the FBI's investigation of college basketball. Now, rock, chalk, Jayhawk fans must sit back and wait untli the NCAA makes their decisions of potential penalties.

Then, there was the wild brawl between bitter rivals Kansas and Kansas State at the end of the Jayhawks' 81-60 victory in Allen Field House. The fight broke out in the disabled seating and included punches, shoving, and at least one player waving a stool. The Jayhawks were dribbling out the time when Silvio De Sousa was stripped by DaJuan Gordon near mid-court. Gordon tried to go for a layup and De Sousa recovered to block his shot and send the freshman sprawling.

DeSousa stood over Gordon and barked at him—triggering both benches to empty. At one point, De Sousa picked up a stool and held it over his head before Kansas assistant Jerrance Howard grabbed it from him from behind. The Jayhawks' Garrett and David McCormick were also in the thick of the scrum along with K-State's James Love and David Sloan. It took both the coaching staffs, the officials, and Allen Field House security to separate the teams.

Afterwards, there were obligatory suspensions and both coaches apologized. Self got all over his team about representing Kansas. There was no call for what transpired. Sometimes you wonder how something like that will affect a team. But they seemed to respond and dedicated themselves to playing with pride.

Kansas went on to take control of the league when the Jayhawks broke Baylor's 23-game winning streak, defeating the Bears, 64-61 in Waco to end Baylor's five-week run as the nation's No. 1 team. Azubuike had 23 points and a career-high 19 rebounds and was too much for the Bears' smaller front line. Azubuike finished his regular season with a career-high 31 points, 14 rebounds and five blocks during a 76-65 Senior Night win over TCU at Allen.

*Bill Self enjoyed his 15th straight season at Kansas with at least 25 wins.*

*Garrett was named Naismith Defensive Player of the Year.*

The Jayhawks tied the Bears in the standings with a 13-1 record, then went on to win their next four games to finish ahead of Baylor by three games. This was their best chance to cut down the nets since defeating Memphis in overtime in 2008 at San Antonio.

"Nobody's had a better season than us," Self said. The Jayhawks had even considered picking the regional in Houston, a right granted to the top overall seed, because the Friday-Sunday games would have given his team an extra day to prepare because Azubuike had been nursing an ankle injury late in the season.

My top trios for the 2019-2020 season:

Kansas: Dotson, Azubuike, Garrett.

Gonzaga: Filip Petrusev, Corey Kispert, Killian Tillie.

Kentucky: Nick Richards, Immanuel Quickley, Tyrese Maxey.

Dayton: Obi Toppin, Jared Crutcher, Rodney Chatman.

Baylor: Jared Butler, Mark Vital, Freddie Gillespie.

# CHAPTER TWO

---

# DAYTON TOPPIN THE CHARTS

One of my first memories of Dayton basketball occurred in 1967, when the Flyers, a perennial Midwest independent power coached by Don Donoher, advanced to the NCAA championship game against UCLA in Louisville.

It was my first trip to the Final Four. I jumped into a car with a couple of buddies, drove to Freedom Hall, and got tickets. The NCAA tournament was a lot different then. March Madness temporarily turned into May Magic when Donnie May dropped 34 points during a 76-62 victory over 4th-ranked North Carolina in the semifinals.

As good as May was, he was no match for the Bruins' iconic 7'1" sophomore center Kareem Abdul-Jabbar, who took his first steps toward immortality when he scored 20 points and grabbed 18 rebounds as UCLA defeated Dayton, in a 79-64 victory for the first of his three national championships.

Fast forward to this season. The program Tom Blackburn and Donoher built, now coached by former Dayton star and alum Anthony Grant, has become one of the feel-good stories of this wild and crazy season. The Flyers jumped up to #3 in the final AP Top 25 regular season poll with a 29-2 record—the best start in school history—and 20 straight victories.

Late in the season, I was scheduled to do the call for Dayton's game against Davidson at the sold-out Dayton Arena. It was a really exciting moment for the fans there, as our ESPN team, consisting of Bob Wischusen, my partner and play-by play man, and superstar sidleine reporter Holly Rowe joined us for the telecast and 13,407 fans filled the University of Dayton Arena. They promoted the game earlier in the week by flashing my face onto the scoreboard. Welcome to the big time, Flyers.

Dayton didn't disappoint. It was really exciting when I was asked to make a major announcement to the fans that *College Gameday* was coming to Dayton the following week. The place went absolutely bananas. It was the first time College Game Day was on campus there.

Against Davidson, the excitement was created by 6'9" high-flying redshirt sophomore star, Obi Toppin, who threw down an assortment of spectacular breakaway dunks. He scored 23 points on 10-of-11 shooting and grabbed 12 rebounds, as the Flyers wrapped up the A-10 regular season with an 82-67 victory. Dayton shot 73 percent, making 27-of-28 two-point field goals as five players scored in double figures. I was impressed by their teamwork.

*Erik Schelkun, Elsestar Images*

*Toppin averaged 20.0 points and 7.5 rebounds a game, shooting .633 pct. from the field.*

Toppin was the best big man this league has seen since Marcus Camby, who led University of Massachusetts to a Final Four in 1996. That team, which defeated eventual-national champion Kentucky in the opening game of the season before losing to the 'Cats in a rematch during the national semifinals, was good enough to win it all that year.

This team was good enough to make a similar run, too, provided they continued to shoot the ball the way they did during the regular season, when they led the country in two-point field goal percentage, making 62.3 percent of their attempts. Four players—Toppin, Trey Landers, Ryan Mikesell, and Iba Watson—attempted more than 100 shots inside the arc and made more than 60 percent of them.

Dayton was a very efficient offensive team, leading the nation in field goal percentage at 52.5 percent. The Flyers were third in the nation in assists per game at 17.6. Their scoring margin was 15.5 points per game, third nationally. Dayton also ranked eighth in assist-to-turnover ratio. They averaged an impressive 80 points per game.

Toppin, a unanimous first team All-American, was a game changer, averaging 20 points and 7.5 rebounds, while shooting 63.3 percent from the field, sixth best in the nation. He showed good range by hitting 39 percent of his trifectas. Jalen Crutcher averaged 15.1 points and just under five assists.

Toppin seemed like an unlikely choice for national Player of the Year before his college career began. He won the Wooden Award and the Naismith Player of the Year, making a meteoric rise this season, letting loose a series of SportsCenter moments. Grant's Flyers burst into the national spotlight, led by Toppin. He averaged 22.3 points, seven rebounds and 2.3 assists, and 1.3 blocked shots in three games, as he led his team to the championship game against Kansas in the Maui Invitational. He then went off for 31 points in a win over North Florida, including a school record 10 dunks.

Toppin became the logical successor to Zion Williamson as the most spectacular dunker in the college game. He had 107 for the season and 24 slams in the final five games alone. "I'm addicted to it," he said. "I didn't start dunking until senior year in high school. I've been dunking everything since."

It wasn't always this easy.

Toppin was born in the Bushwick section of Brooklyn, the son of street ball legend Obadiah Toppin, another monster dunker who played for Globe Institute N.Y. The father later flourished professionally in basketball's minor leagues, and he introduced his son to the game at the local parks where he picked up the nickname, "The Next Generation."

*Toppin stops by to say hello.*
*Dayton defeated Davidson that evening.*

Toppin moved to Florida for family reasons and started high school there before he, his mother, and his younger brother moved back to Westchester County, where he struggled to get playing time as a 6'2" junior at Ossining, (New York) High School. Toppin only played one season of varsity basketball. Despite averaging 20.6 points, 8.1 rebounds, three assists, and three steals as a 6'5" senior, and leading his team to its first conference championship in 10 years, Toppin did not receive a Division I offer and opted to enroll at Mt. Zion Prep in Baltimore, where he averaged 17 points, eight rebounds, and four assists and—most importantly—grew four more inches.

Toppin committed to play for Dayton, over Georgetown and Rhode Island, and—after being ineligible as a freshman—he started to make his presence felt, averaging 14.4 points and 5.6 rebounds. He became the first player since Lamar Odom in 1999 to be named Atlantic 10 Rookie of the Year and first team All-Conference. He toyed with the idea of declaring for the NBA draft and worked out for several teams before deciding to return to school.

College basketball is glad he did!

Dayton was one of biggest surprises in college basketball. The Flyers were coming off a 21-win season that ended with a first round NIT loss at Colorado. They were picked to finish third in the preseason A-10 poll behind VCU and Davidson, receiving just one first place vote from the 28 head coaches and media who participated. Aside from Toppin, Dayton's second-best player, junior Crutcher,

*Jalen Crutcher led Dayton in minutes played (33.7 per game) and assists (148).*

was a point guard from Memphis who was overlooked by his hometown team. Grant, who had been highly successful at VCU a decade ago, made just one NCAA tournament in the last eight seasons as head coach at Alabama and Dayton.

But Grant put the Flyers in position to become a first seed in the tournament after the Flyers were the only team in the country that did not lose a game in regulation. Dayton's only losses came in overtime on neutral sites—to Kansas in Maui and to Colorado at the Chicago Legends event.

*Anthony Grant is the first coach to win Naismith Coach of the Year while coaching at his alma mater since Jim Boeheim in 2010.*

# CHAPTER THREE

# FLORIDA STATE HAS ITS OWN PERFORMANCE OF (LEONARD) HAMILTON

I've been impressed by the way Leonard Hamilton has built up his program in Tallahassee.

The Florida State coach had his one shining moment as an assistant at Kentucky, under Joe B. Hall in 1978, when the Wildcats won a national championship.

Now, at the age of 71, Hamilton figured to be running out of chances to win a title of his own. This 2019-2020 season could have been his best chance for a breakthrough tournament.

Despite losing three starters, Hamilton, an exceptional recruiter, had experience, quality, and depth in a senior point guard and four-year starter Trent Forrest, the size with two useable seven-footers could win the ACC regular season outright over Duke, Virginia, and Louisville. The fourth-ranked Seminoles were 26-5 overall and 16-4 in one of the toughest conferences in the country.

*Leonard Hamilton is 55-13 over the last two seasons.*

*Ross Obley*

*Devin Vassell led the Seminoles in scoring last season (12.7 ppg.).*

They were close last season, winning 29 games and advancing to the Sweet 16, a year after they reached the Elite Eight.

"That's what our plan was," Hamilton said. "We felt from the beginning—and from the end of last year—that we had a team coming back that could compete for the national championship."

Hamilton won the ACC's Coach of the Year, an honor he won in 2009 and 2012, when the Seminoles won a piece of the ACC regular season title; and was a finalist for the Naismith national Coach of the Year. If Hamilton's team would have won it all, he would become the first black coach to win a national title since Connecticut's Kevin Ollie in 2014. The short list also includes John Thompson of Georgetown in 1984, Nolan Richardson of Arkansas in 1994, and Tubby Smith of Kentucky in 1998.

It takes on special significance when you realize that, at the beginning of the season, there were only 14 black head coaches in the 75 programs in college basketball's six major conferences. And if you only consider the Power 5 conferences, the number drops to 13.8 percent, given the Big East has five black coaches. Now compare that to the fact that 80 percent of major-conference scholarship basketball players are black and you start to see why coaches like Hamilton and their accomplishments have become such a big deal.

Hamilton has always been a pioneer. He grew up poor in Gastonia, North Carolina, in the segregated South. His mother was a domestic worker and his father was a truck driver.

He was the first black player at UT-Martin; he was a walk-on who then became team captain. He was the first black assistant at Kentucky and the first black head coach in the Big 12 when he took the Oklahoma State job in 1989. He reinvented basketball at Miami, a program that had been dormant from 1971 through 1985, and he did so with no conference affiliation or on-campus gym.

Now, Hamilton has built a national power at Florida State, a football school. He has been at Florida State for 18 years. He is the school's all-time winningest coach and the fifth winningest coach in ACC history with 170 victories, behind Mike Krzyzewski, Dean Smith, Roy Williams, and Gary Williams of Maryland.

FSU has won 23 straight home games. The 2020 Seminoles had more options, and Hamilton was not afraid to use all of them, playing upwards to 12-a-game to wear down opposing teams that were top heavy with superstars. The Seminoles are 36-8 in ACC games decided by one possession or overtime wins since 2012.

"We win by *committee* and most teams feature *people*," Hamilton said. "We don't feature one particular person. We let the game come to them. We have a system where we get everybody involved. I think that makes us more challenging to play. The go-to person is the guy with the highest percentage shot. Our guys all feel equal. We don't have a Zion Williamson that makes you [media] guys tickle your fancy. We're not quite as sexy. We are different. We're not like everybody else."

Hamilton's players are talented, but unselfish. The Seminoles' leading scorer was 6'6" sophomore guard Devin Vassell, who averaged 12.7 points and was a second team All-ACC, along with Forrest. Then add 6'5" junior wing guard M.J. Walker who averaged over 10 points, while 6'9" freshman forward Patrick Williams, the player with the highest NBA draft ceiling, came off the bench to average 9.2 points. Hamilton was able to blend them into a rotation that included two seven-footers—7'0", 260-pound, Ole Miss transfer Dominik Olejniczak, and 7'1", 240-pound, Balsa Kopriva; both shot over 61 percent.

*Trent Forrest led Florida State in assists (124). He shot 82.2 pct. from the foul line.*

*M.J. Walker averaged 10.6 ppg.*

"This team has set a standard by which all Florida State teams will be judged," Hamilton said. "They had tremendous chemistry that allowed them to win big despite not necessarily being the most talented team we've had here."

Florida State beat its share of good teams—defeating Louisville twice, Notre Dame, Florida, Purdue, and the defending national champion Virginia, shooting 37 percent from the three and winning six of its final seven games to win their first conference championship since 1993 (when they were still a member of the old Metro Conference).

*Malik Osborne.*

It's hard to predict what might have happened in March Madness. But the Florida State Senate passed a resolution proclaiming the Seminoles, *"Champions by Default."* The resolution said it would be presented to Hamilton and university president John Thrasher "…as a tangible token of the sentiments of Florida State."

"We may not be blue bloods," Hamilton said. "But we are new blood. That's us. Seminoles."

Florida State had a season to be proud of. It could have been even greater if the big dance had been held.

*Patrick Williams.*

The Seminoles set a school-record for ACC wins. Here are the most conference wins:

|  | W-L |
|---|---|
| 2019-2020 | 16-4 |
| 2018-2019 | 13-5 |
| 2011-2012 | 12-4 |
| 1992-1993 | 12-4 |
| 2016-2017 | 12-6 |

# CHAPTER FOUR

# BAYLOR'S ONE SHINING MOMENT

Baylor's magical season may have ended prematurely, but Bears' coach Scott Drew chose to celebrate one of his program's best years yet by producing a personalized version of "One Shining Moment." It was a fitting way to honor a fifth-ranked 26-4 team that won a Big 12 record 23 straight games, finally defeated Kansas at Allen Field House, and spent five consecutive weeks as No. 1 in the AP Top 25. There was an endless series of highlights from a team that most likely would have been a No. 1 seed in an NCAA tournament.

Drew admitted that his wife, Kelly, started crying the first time she watched the three-minute video. He had a different take. "I was more just feeling proud," he said during a post-season conference call. "You're watching it and it's like 'Wow, we had a great season. These guys really accomplished a lot of stuff.' It was really enjoyable. Some seasons are a little more of a grind than others. This season, it seemed like every day was fun going to work. No matter win or lose, these guys were always in the gym, they were always energetic, and they were always fun to coach. You don't find that a lot of times in society."

Drew has been at Baylor for 17 years. When he first arrived, the program had been rocked by the darkest scandal in school history. In August 2003, Dave Bliss resigned after the arrest of one of his players, Carlton Dotson, for the murder of teammate Patrick Dennehy. Bliss attempted to cover up the under-the-table payments he had made in violation of NCAA rules. The coach smeared Dennehy's name by suggesting Dennehy obtained the money by dealing drugs.

The team Drew inherited was so bad, many of Baylor's best players transferred and the new coach had to search the campus for potential walk-ons so he could practice.

It took Drew five years to get the program up and running. When he signed three McDonald's

Baylor University

*Freddie Gillespie went from Division III to Baylor stardom.*

All-Americans—Perry Jones III, Quincy Miller, and Isaiah Austin—as well as other Top 100 recruits Baylor barely got in the past. Other Big 12 coaches privately grew suspicious about his ambitious recruiting tactics.

Drew coached the Bears to a pair of Elite Eights in 2010 and 2012, but complaints led to the NCAA investigation that uncovered modest violations like impermissible calls and texts from assistant coaches to recruits that resulted in a two-game suspension for Drew.

Drew shouldered on, winning at least 18 games a year for 12 straight seasons.

Scott Drew has been maligned throughout his career. People say he's got players, but he can't really coach. He's done an amazing job when you think about it. Take a look at what he stepped into…that Dave Bliss situation was unbelievable. It was a total nightmare down there. He came in and he changed that whole culture.

He's got a great personality, exceptional work ethic, and super energy. I spent a lot of time with him before their game against Florida in Gainesville. I was really impressed. He has tremendous rapport with his players. He has great kids who are all about the team. This all started with the guy up top running the show. Anybody who wants to knock him, to me, they're talking to the wrong guy. His team played with a chip on their shoulder. They weren't big-time recruits who were wined and dined.

Drew became a logical candidate for national Coach of the Year after squeezing the most from these Bad News Bears, which had no McDonald's All-Americans or one-and-done first round NBA draft picks on its roster. This is not the way your national contender normally looks.

"The type of people on the team aren't the usual five-star highly recruited athletes," sophomore point guard Jared Butler said, "We've got all these guys who did not have anything given to them. And now these guys are looking for blood. When I say people are in the gym constantly, it's one of the most competitive things I've ever been around."

Butler has emerged as the star of this team, which was ranked 16th in the AP's preseason poll, then exceeded expectations. He was a first team All-Big 12 selection, a third team AP All-American, and finalist for the Bob Cousy award after averaging 16.0 points, 3.2 rebounds, 3.1 assists, and 1.6 steals. He carried this team of gym rats and overachievers to new heights after 6'10" Tristan Clark, the team's second-leading scorer in 2019, did not make a complete comeback from his 2019 season-ending knee injury. The team was also missing 6'8" junior forward Mario Kegler, an honorable mention All-Big 12 choice the previous year, who was suspended for a violation of team rules and dropped out of school with the intention of turning pro.

Butler didn't know it at the time, but he was destined to play for Drew from the time he was an 11-year old chubby-cheeked-kid. He grew up in Reserve, Louisiana, the same hometown as former Baylor players Rico Gathers and Tweety Carter. Butler was attending a game between Riverside Academy and New Orleans prep power St. Augustine, when his father Richard convinced him to ask Drew, who was in the gym to recruit Gathers, if he would pose for a picture with his son.

Drew, of course, said yes.

Richard Butler saved the photo on his phone, then stored it on his computer. Seven years later, he showed it to Drew when the coach made an in-home visit to recruit the younger Butler, who had grown eight inches and turned into one of the Louisiana Players of the Year. Butler's final three schools were Virginia, Baylor, and Alabama.

He initially committed to Alabama. He was confused as to why Baylor didn't recruit him harder, given the fact he attended the same high school as Gathers and Carter and because his coach, Tim Byrd, was close friends with Drew.

"It seemed weird that I wasn't getting recruited by Baylor until late," Butler said "So I thought maybe they didn't want me as much. I was told later they were short on scholarships and long on guards. I don't know why I took it personally, but I did."

Butler enrolled at Alabama in July, but didn't participate in team workouts. The next month, a scholarship opened up at

*Baylor University*

*Jared Butler was a unanimous All-Big 12 First-Team honoree.*

Baylor due to the early retirement of Jake Lindsey. Butler requested an unconditional release from his commitment to Alabama, so he could transfer to Baylor and he received a waiver so he could play as a freshman.

He made the All-Big 12 Newcomer team as a freshman. Then, his career took off. Butler was selected MVP after the Bears defeated Villanova to win the Myrtle Beach Invitational in November. Butler scored 22 points as Baylor defeated Kansas for its first win at Allen Field House en route to winning its first 14 games in conference play, before losing two of their last three.

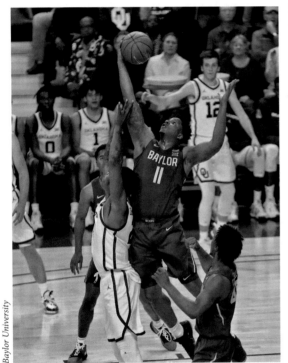

Baylor University

*Vital was a Naismith Defensive Player of the Year finalist.*

Baylor's other four top scorers were all transfers.

Redshirt junior guard MaCio Teague was a former two-time All-Big South selection from UNC-Asheville who left when Coach Nick McDevitt left for Middle Tennessee State. Sophomore guard Davion Mitchell was a four-star recruit at Auburn who transferred for more playing time. Senior guard Devonte Bandoo, the team's sixth man, was a 1,000-point scorer from Hutchinson (Kansas Community College); and 6'8" senior redshirt forward, Freddie Gillespie, was a former preferred walk-on from Division III Carleton (Minnesota) College who earned a scholarship.

That group of gym rats and 6'5" junior wing Mark Vital, a finalist for national defensive Player of the Year, combined to build one of the best resumés in the country.

The chemistry was so good that Drew was selected Big 12 Coach of the Year and all five starters made one of the All Big 12 teams for the first time in its 24-year history. Three of those starters—Mitchell, Vital, and Gillespie—made the all-defensive team. Gillespie was Most Improved Player. Mitchell was the Newcomer of the Year and both he and Teague, who averaged 13.9 points, were unanimous choices for the All-Newcomers' team.

The Bears, who had the third most wins in program history, impressed in non-conference play, defeating Villanova, Arizona, Butler, and Florida, then dominated the Big 12. They had the best record against Top 25 teams with a 6-1 record, making their case as a No. 1 regional seed with a nation's best

11-2 record in NET Quadrant I games. The Bears were second in the number of Quadrant I wins to Kansas, which had 12. Every other team with 10 plus Quadrant I wins had at least six QI losses. Three of Baylor's four losses to Washington, Kansas, and TCU, were by three points each.

The Bears won big with defense. Baylor ranked seventh nationally in scoring defense, giving up just 60.1 points per game, and 18th nationally in scoring margin of 11 points. Their defensive scoring average was just shy of the Big 12 scoring defense record (59.4 by Texas A & M in 2007). The Bears held opponents to a 39.7 field goal percentage and 31.1 percent on three-pointers.

Baylor was one of seven teams to hold down the top spot in the weekly AP poll during the 2019-2020 season:

Michigan State

Kentucky

Duke

Kansas

Louisville

Gonzaga

Baylor

# CHAPTER FIVE

# GONZAGA CONTENDS AGAIN

I was very impressed with the second-ranked Zags (31-2, 15-1 in WCC) when I called the WCC tournament in Vegas, beating St. Mary's, 84-66, in the championship game to win their eighth title in 10 years and 18th overall. It marked the 23rd straight time the Zags were in the WCC title game, an amazing statistic. Gonzaga was a likely No. 1 NCAA Tournament seed. They were a #1 seed in 2013, 2017, and 2019. Yes, that conference tournament was completed before the shutdown, and Mark Few told me next year's team will be better.

Few should know. He has been the head coach at Gonzaga since 1999, a year when the Bulldogs made a Cinderella run to the Elite Eight, and has led the Bulldogs to the NCAA Tournament in every season during his tenure. Few has served on the coaching staff since 1989 and has been a constant throughout a period where the Zags established themselves as a major basketball power playing in a mid-major conference. Gonzaga has appeared in every final AP poll since the 2008-2009 season and enjoyed their best season in school history in 2016-2017 when they won 37 games and went to their first Final Four, advancing to the national championship game.

*Gonzaga Athletics*

*Few had his 13th straight season with at least 25 wins.*

When I look at the créme de la créme programs across America, Few's team is high on the list. He has built something special, and they will contend year in and year out.

Few was selected national Coach of the Year in 2017, and he and assistant Tommy Lloyd have built this program with resourceful overseas recruiting.

When talking about successful programs across America, Few has built one of the most consistent. Think about some of these numbers:

With the win in the WCC tournament, the Zags locked up a 22nd straight trip to the big dance. They were ranked #1 nationally for the fifth time in program history. Gonzaga won 20 or more games for the 23rd straight season. The program enjoyed its sixth 30-win season and the 13th straight year with at least 25 wins.

I also saw the Zags in one of their most exciting games of the year, a 73-72 OT win over Oregon in the Battle4Atlantis. I called the tournament final when they lost to Michigan, 82-64. That was the only time Gonzaga was held under 70 points all season.

Gonzaga lost just once the rest of the season, a 91-78 setback at BYU.

Gonzaga Athletics

*Tillie had an injury-plagued career but success on the court for the Zags.*

The Zags had so much depth and talent as six players averaged double figures in scoring. There was 6'10" valuable senior Killian Tillie from France, who had an injury-plagued career; 6'11" sophomore WCC Player of the Year Filip Petrusev from Belgrade, Serbia, and 6'7" junior wing Corey Kispert. Petrusev did not start a single game as a freshman, but became the team's featured scorer last year, averaging 17.5 points and 7.9 rebounds while drawing a ridiculous 8.5 fouls per 40 minutes in WCC games. He scored 20 or more points 11 times, including a 31-point effort against Santa Clara, hitting 14-of-18 field goals.

Kispert averaged just under 14 points and made 44 percent of his three-point attempts. He shined vs. North Carolina, scoring 26 points, hitting 10-of-12 field goals, including 5-of-6 trifectas.

The Zags led the nation in scoring last year, averaging 87.4 points, and their offensive efficiency was outstanding.

Gonzaga had other solid contributors like 6'5" sophomore Joel Ayayi from Bordeaux, France. Ayayi averaged 10.6 points per game, shot 82.5 percent from the foul line, and scored 17 points in the WCC Championship win over Saint Mary's. There was so much talent as the backcourt included graduate transfers Admon Gilder (10.7 ppg.) and Ryan Woolridge (10.1 ppg., 4.2 apg.).

Having Petrusev and 6'10" freshman Drew Timme (9.8 points per game last season) up front was exceptional. Timme, who scored 15 of his 17 points in the first half of the Zags' conference title game against St. Mary's, will be even better with a greater role next season. I really loved him when I watched him. Then add 6'8" freshman Anton Watson, who showed potential before being injured.

The Gonzaga team was deep and much improved after the Bulldogs played a seven-man rotation for the latter half of the season. The cancellation of the season ended the chance at the elusive national title. They will be a contender to cut down the nets at the end of the 2020-21 season.

Gonzaga ranked in the top 10 nationally in numerous categories:

|  | Rank | Stat |
|---|---|---|
| Scoring offense | 1st | 87.4 ppg. |
| Scoring margin | 1st | +19.6 pts. |
| W-L percentage | 1st | 93.9 pct. |
| Field Goal Pct. | 2nd | 51.5 pct. |
| Rebound margin | 4th | +9.2 |
| Asst.-to-TO ratio. | 4th | 1.49-1 |
| Assists per game. | 7th | 16.7 apg. |
| 3-pt. FG percentage | 8th | 38.6 pct. |

# CHAPTER SIX

# SAN DIEGO STATE SURPRISES THE NATION

San Diego State has always been an undervalued program on the West Coast. But the Mountain West Aztecs, under Steve Fisher and former assistant/second-year head coach, Brian Dutcher, decided to honor one of their best players ever—2019 NBA Finals MVP Kawhi Leonard. This season, they flew Leonard's No. 15 jersey in the rafters of Viejas Arena.

Leonard helped lead the Aztecs to a 34-3 record in the 2010-2011 season, when they advanced to the NCAA Sweet 16, before losing a close game to eventual national champion, Connecticut. That Aztecs team may have been the greatest in school history.

This year's San Diego State team had another chance to make history when the Aztecs won their first 26 games of the season. They built their resumé with non-league victories over BYU, Creighton, and Iowa, three teams that would have been in the tournament.

The last team to go undefeated through a regular season was St. Joseph's, which went 28-0 in 2004. The last team to *finish* the year undefeated was the 1976 Bob Knight-led Indiana team with Scott May, Kent Benson, and Quinn Buckner.

San Diego State was headed in that direction…before the Aztecs were stunned at home by UNLV, 66-63, on Feb. 22. The Aztecs went 30-2, including 17-1 in conference play. They were on the verge of a No. 1 seed before they were upset by Utah State in the Mountain West championship game. Let's face it, San Diego State did not figure on this type of success when the season started. Utah State was the preseason conference favorite.

*Dutcher led the Aztecs to 26 straight wins to start the season.*

I talked with Dutcher, and he told me he went the route of recruiting older transfers. He said, "Dick, we thought that was the best option for us, instead of going for some high school kids." And he was right. That's the new trend we have in basketball. A lot of the players are one and done, but they are fifth-year graduate transfers.

Dutcher, who coached the Aztecs to 21 wins and the Mountain West Conference tournament championship in 2019, upgraded his roster around three key transfers—established scoring guards KJ Feagin and Malachi Flynn and 6'10" forward Yanni Wetzell. He surrounded them with junior forward Matt Mitchell (12.2 points, 4.8 rebounds), a three-year starter; 6'10" sophomore forward Nathan Mensah (6.9 points, 6.8 rebounds), and 6'8" three-point shooting junior wing Jordan Schakel (10.0 points).

Flynn, a 6'1" junior from Tacoma, Washington, joined the team from Washington State. There, he averaged 15.8 points and 4.3 assists for the Pac-12 as a sophomore, but toiled in obscurity for two years. He was a second team AP All-American and was the only transfer on the top three All-American teams. He led San Diego State in scoring with 17.5 points, 4.5 rebounds, and 5.1 assists, shooting 92 percent from the line in conference games.

"To do it as a transfer is incredible," Dutcher said. "How many transfers achieve that in their first year of eligibility at their new school?"

6'1" Feagin, who averaged 17.5 points and 4.0 assists as a junior at Santa Clara, arrived after he broke his foot in the second game of his senior season. Facing six weeks of rehab and knowing he eventually needed foot surgery, Feagin opted to take a medical redshirt and play his final season elsewhere, after three losing seasons. He chose San Diego

*Malachi Flynn.*

State over Oregon. He averaged 9.1 points, sacrificing his scoring to become a defensive stopper.

Wetzell was a foreign import from Auckland, New Zealand, who averaged 5.9 points for Vanderbilt even while, five years earlier, he was a tennis player with a junior world ranking. After the SEC Commodores suffered through a winless 0-18 conference season in 2019, Wetzell committed to the Aztecs over Texas Tech. He gave San Diego State some much needed size, while averaging 11.6 points and 6.5 rebounds per game.

*Flynn led the Aztecs in scoring (17.5 ppg.) and assists (5.1 apg.).*

Winning was a new experience for all three transfer players. The Aztecs made an immediate impact when they rallied to win at BYU in the season's second game, only their fourth win there in 33 tries. Then they won the Las Vegas Invitational, beating Big East power Creighton by 31 points and rallying from 16 down to beat Iowa. Dutcher's team relied on solid defense. The Aztecs were ranked third nationally in scoring defense, giving up just 59.4 points per game. They were third in scoring margin at 15.4 points and No. 13 in three-point field goal percentage at 38 percent.

San Diego State entered the Top 10 in January. The program's 10-week run inside the Top 10 of the AP Top 25 was the second-longest in program history and trails only the 13-week streak from December 10, 2010, through March 14, 2011. The Aztecs' No. 6 ranking in both the AP and Coaches Poll was the third highest in school history and made Dutcher a legitimate national Coach of the Year candidate.

San Diego State was one of six teams to hold opponents to less than 60 points per game:

Virginia—52.4

Liberty—53.8

San Diego State—59.4

Vermont—59.5

Sacramento State—59.7

New Mexico State—59.7

# CHAPTER SEVEN

# THE SENIORS

## Winston, Howard, Pritchard, Powell, Azubuike Led the Way

When the announcement came down that the NCAA was cancelling the tournament, one of the first reactions was the shocking end of so many careers. There were quality seniors who saw any chance of listening to "One Shining Moment" taken away. They also had any shot of a conference tournament title erased as well.

Think about some of the senior stars that were ready to shine: Guard Myles Powell of Seton Hall, guard Markus Howard of Marquette, point guard Payton Pritchard of Oregon, point guard Cassius Winston of Michigan State, and Kansas' center Udoka Azubuike all saw their dreams taken away.

They all had great careers and All-American seasons. All wiped out so quickly. It was an especially tough season for Winston who lost his younger brother earlier in the season.

Think about what these guys meant to their programs.

Powell was a first team AP All-American who was selected Big East Player of the Year after averaging 21 points, 4.3 rebounds, and 2.9 per game while receiving the most attention on the defensive end from the opponents. He surpassed the 2,000-point milestone for a team that finished in a three-way tie for the regular season

*Powell passed the 2,000-point plateau.*

*Powell averaged 21 ppg. for the Pirates.*

championship for the first time since 1993. In the second game of the season against Stony Brook, Powell suffered a serious ankle injury, but proceeded to play in the next game against Michigan State, scoring 37 points during a 76-73 loss at the Rock. On Dec. 14, Powell suffered a concussion during a loss at Rutgers and was ruled out indefinitely. He returned after missing two games and had 27 points, five rebounds, and five steals in a 74-66 win over DePaul.

Powell is a self-made player who grew up in rough-and-tumble Trenton. He was one of the best shooters in the country and might have been ranked in the Top 25 as a senior with South Kent School, if he hadn't put on extra weight after suffering a foot injury. Powell signed at the Hall, picking the local school over seven other offers, including Pittsburgh, Rutgers, Cincinnati, and Connecticut. He reported to the Hall weighing 250 pounds and proceeded to lose 50 pounds by changing his diet and turning into a gym rat who averaged double figures for four years.

The 5'11" Howard, a first team AP All-American from Gilbert, Arizona, was the nation's leading scorer, averaging 27.8 points. He set the Big East single-season record for scoring average (28.7) in Big East games, breaking the previous record of 27.8 points per game set by Boston College's Troy Bell in 2003. Howard has been a relentless offensive threat for four years, becoming Marquette's all-time leading scorer when he torched Loyola, Maryland, for 39 points in the season opener. On Nov. 29, Howard scored 51 points in a 101-79 victory over USC. He became the third player to score 50 points in a game in three straight seasons, joining Wayman Tisdale and Pete Maravich.

Howard, whose older brother Jordan is the all-time leading scorer at Central Arkansas, has gotten better every season. As a sophomore, he averaged 20.7 points with a 52-point explosion in overtime at Providence. He averaged 25 points and was selected Big East Player of the Year as a junior when he had a pair of 45-point showings—including 40 in the

*Markus Howard led the nation in scoring (27.8 ppg.) and three-pointers made per game (4.17).*

second half against Buffalo—and a program-record 53-point performance at Creighton. On Feb. 12, Howard scored 24 points in a 72-71 loss to Villanova, becoming the Big East's all-time leading scorer in league games, surpassing Lawrence Moten's 1,405 points.

Over the course of his last five outings, Howard scored at least 30 points every game, averaging 33.2 points and shooting 49 percent and 50 percent from three-point range. At the end of the season, he was selected as unanimous first team All-Big East and finished with 2,761 points during his career.

The 6'2" Pritchard, a first team AP All-American, was a local hero who was selected Pac-12 Player of the Year after leading the Ducks to a 24-7 record, including a 17-0 mark at home, and the conference regular season championship. Pritchard, who led West Linn (Oregon) High to four consecutive state championships and earned the 2014 and 2015 Todd Pratt Player of the Year award, averaged 20.5 points, 5.6 assists, and 4.3 rebounds, setting school records for assists (659), wins (105), games played (144).

Pritchard initially committed to Oklahoma, where his father Terry played football, then changed his mind and signed with the Ducks. In his greatest game in high

*Payton Pritchard was named Pac-12 Player of the Year.*

Oregon Athletic Communications

school, Pritchard torched Washington for 45 in the Northwest Shootout, an all-star game between the two Northwest states. He was a four-year starter who was named MVP of the Pac-12 tournament and led the Ducks to a surprise Sweet 16 appearance. Pritchard declared for the 2019 NBA draft but decided to return to Oregon for his senior year, punctuating his final season with a career-high 38 points in a 73-72 win against Arizona in February.

6'1" Winston, the former Detroit Jesuit High star, won the Big Ten Player of the Year and was an AP first team All-American as a junior. He thought about declaring for the NBA draft after that year, then had a change of heart and decided to follow in the footprints of Magic Johnson in 1978 and also Mateen Cleaves in 1999. Winston opted to return to school for one more year to try to win a national championship. Michigan State entered the season as preseason number one in the AP poll.

Winston averaged 18.6 points, 5.9 assists, 2.5 rebounds, and 1.2 steals in 32.7 minutes a game. He shot 44.8 percent, including 43.2 percent from three-point range, and made 85.2 percent of his free

*Cassius Winston averaged 18.6 ppg. and 5.9 apg. during his senior season.*

throws to lead the Spartans to a 22-9 overall record and a share of a third consecutive Big Ten regular season title. He was a unanimous All-Big Ten selection for a second straight year and a consensus second-team All-American who finished with 1,969 career points and a school record 894 assists.

The 7'0", 267-pound Azubuike, with his 7'7" wingspan, was the youngest of five children born to a police officer and a middle school teacher in Lagos, Nigeria. He caught the attention of recruiters with Basketball Without Borders and was offered a scholarship to play basketball at Potter's House Christian Academy in Jacksonville, Florida, despite not playing a game until he was 13. He was an immediate success on and off the court, making the 2016 McDonald's All-American game and then signing with Kansas over Florida State and North Carolina.

Azubuike entered school as an overweight freshman but was ready for the NBA by the end of his sophomore year in 2018. He might have left at the end of his junior year if he hadn't suffered a season ending torn ligament in his right hand in January of 2019. As a senior, he was selected Big 12 Player of the Year and AP second-team All-American after averaging 13.7 points, 10.5 rebounds, and 2.6 blocks, finishing with a career field goal percentage of 74.9 percent, the highest in NCAA history.

Azubuike came up huge in the biggest games. He scored a career-high 29 points in a 90-84 overtime win against Dayton in Maui; then scored 23 points and a career-high 19 rebounds in a 64-61 win over top-ranked Baylor in Waco.

Other seniors to keep an eye on in March included: guard Anthony Cowan, Jr., Maryland; forward Lamar Stevens, Penn State; forward Yoeli Childs, BYU; guard Sam Merrill, Utah State; guard Kamar Baldwin, Butler; forward Mamadi Diakite, Virginia;

*Kansas' center Udoka Azubuike scored 29 points in an OT win over Dayton.*

forward Kristian Doolittle, Oklahoma; guard Zavier Simpson, Michigan; forward Kerry Blackshear, Florida; guard-forward Alpha Diallo, Providence; guard Trent Forrest, Florida State, and guard Jarron Cumberland, Cincinnati.

These guys were special and their NCAA careers ended so abruptly. I enjoyed watching all of them and know they had special performances ahead in the big dance that never happened.

Here are the top career scorers at the end of the 2019-20 season, all seniors:

Markus Howard, Marquette.    2761

Jermaine Marrow, Hampton.   2680

Grant Riller, Charleston        2474

Charles Williams, Howard.     2404

Jerrick Harding, Weber St.      2266

Myles Powell, Seton Hall        2252

Tres Tinkle, Oregon St.          2233

Lamar Stevens, Penn St.        2207

# CHAPTER EIGHT

# MID-MAJORS BREAKTHROUGH

## Liberty and East Tennessee State Shine

The term "mid-major" has always been interesting to me. If you are not a member of a Power 5 conference, are you a mid-major? Does Villanova, a member of the Big East, fall into that category after the Wildcats won two NCAA titles in 2016 and 2018? Of course not.

Is Gonzaga really a mid-major? The Zags may play in the West Coast Conference, but they are a perennial Top 10 team and a national contender that has already played in a national championship game in 2017 so that description doesn't fit.

I know the fans and the media love Cinderella stories, and the big dance provides the opportunity for the Davids of the college basketball world to provide shock city to the Goliaths on neutral sites.

Over the years think about Butler. In 2010 and 2011, the Bulldogs, under Brad Stevens' leadership, reached the title game as a representative of the Horizon League and America's underdog. Butler lost to Duke, 61-59, in a game that went to the wire and could have gone the other way if Gordon Hayward's half-court shot, which hit the backboard, then rim, had dropped through the net in hometown Indianapolis. The next year, Butler showed it was not a fluke, advancing to the finals again before losing to Jim Calhoun's Connecticut Huskies, 53-41. That was a Final Four in Houston that also featured VCU from the Atlantic 10, which upset top-seed Kansas in its regional final.

Think about what Coach Jim Larrañaga, (now at Miami) and former coach of George Mason accomplished in 2006. The 11th-seeded Patriots, a commuter school from Fairfax, Virginia, that received a much-criticized at-large bid out of the Colonial Athletic Association, upset Michigan State, North Carolina, and top-seeded Connecticut to advance to the Final Four. March 26 became an historic date when Mason took down the highly-favored Huskies. The Patriots were raining threes in the second half to rally from nine down to take down the Big East Huskies, 86-84, in overtime at the Verizon Center in

*Dakota Hamilton/ETSU Photos.*

*Steve Forbes led ETSU to a school-record 30 wins. He left for Wake Forest after the season.*

Washington, D.C., to reach the Promised Land.

Players like Jai Lewis, who scored 20 points, Regional MVP Lamar Butler, and Tony Skinn became instant stars and had a week to bask in the spotlight. They came back to earth when Florida, an SEC team with future NBA stars Al Horford and Joakim Noah, made a dozen threes during a 73-57 win in the national semifinals in Indianapolis.

During the 2019-20 season, a growing number of mid-majors impressed and punched tickets to the big dance. Headlining that group were a pair of 30-win teams, East Tennessee State and Liberty.

For the second time in the last four years, ETSU qualified for the NCAA tournament, completing a school-record 30-4 season with a 72-58 win over Wofford in the 100th Southern Conference tournament championship game. Senior guard Isaiah Tisdale was selected MVP after scoring 24 points for the Bucs, who were 16-2 in league play, went 16-1 at home, and finished with a 12-game winning streak.

Steve Forbes is a coach on the rise. He had a 130-43 record at ETSU in five years and his teams play lockdown defense. The numbers didn't lie as they limited 16 of 19 Southern Conference opponents to less than 70 points, surrendering just 63.3 points during double-digit wins over VMI, Western Carolina, and Wofford in tournament play. Forbes benefited big time from his success at ETSU, as he became Head Coach of Wake Forrest, and joined the prestigious ACC.

In addition to Tisdale, senior guard Tray Boyd III and sophomore guard Daivien Williamson also made the all-tournament team. Boyd and Williamson were both voted first team All-Southern Conference, and the Bucs got an added plus when 6-7 forward Jeromy Rodriguez, who flirted with the pros, decided to come back to school.

Grandma and grandpa would have loved this sleeper in

*Tom Raymond*

*Coach Forbes with Isaiah Tisdale.*

their bracket. If you think East Tennessee State wasn't worthy of consideration, go ask Will Wade. LSU lost a home game to the Bucs, 74-63, during the regular season.

Ritchie McKay had things rolling at Liberty. After spending six years as an assistant to Tony Bennett at Virginia, he returned to the private Christian university in Lynchburg, Virginia, for a second stint as head coach in 2015. McKay built the Atlantic Sun program up to a point where they won 29 games in 2019 and 30 in 2020, making the NCAA tournament in both seasons. The Flames lit up the Vine Center in its final year, going 17-0.

*Joe Mihalich led Hofstra to a 26-8 record and a CAA Tournament title.*

Caleb Homesley, a 6'6" senior guard with ACC skills, was named ASUN Player of the Year and MVP of the conference tournament after scoring 26 points and grabbing eight rebounds in a 66-62 semi-final win over Stetson. He had 16 points and nine boards in a 73-58 victory over Lipscomb in the championship game. Both he and 6'8" junior forward Scottie James, a one-time transfer from Bradley, both could have received more ink with added exposure in the big dance.

There were others who were worth a look, like Hofstra and Winthrop, who already secured NCAA bids.

Joe Mihalich's 26-8 Hofstra Pride won the Colonial Athletic Association for the first time since Jay Wright did the trick in 2001. This year's squad had a win over UCLA in Westwood early in the season. Mihalich found a way to replace record-setting guard Justin Wright-Foreman, getting the most out of senior point guard Desure Buie, who averaged 18.2 points; and 6'5" senior swingman Eli Pemberton, who averaged 17.6 points and had 12 of his 19 points in the second half as the Pride rallied to defeat Northeastern, 70-61, in the finals in Washington, D.C.

Freshman DJ Burns scored 12 of his 16 points in the second half as second-seeded Winthrop overcame a 15-point deficit to capture its

*Desure Buie averaged 18.2 ppg, and 5.9 apg. for Hofstra.*

11<sup>th</sup> Big South Conference title with a 78-68 victory over fifth-seeded Hampton. The Eagles, coached by Pat Kelsey, won 24 games for just the fourth time in program history.

On Selection Sunday, the mid-majors were among the schools most thrilled to hear their names called and the announcement of where they were going.

They were ready to face the big boys. But they had that moment taken away. Another sad reality.

Let's salute the East Tennessee States and the Libertys, schools that could have created excitement in the big dance.

# CHAPTER NINE

# KENTUCKY REVITALIZATION

Big Blue nation was expecting big things from Kentucky at the start of the 2019-20 season.

Don't they always. It always seems to be Final Four or bust in the Commonwealth and this year seemed no different. The SEC Wildcats were coming off a 30-7 Elite Eight season that ended with a loss to Auburn in the Midwest Regional final. With the losses of sophomore forward PJ Washington and two freshmen, guard Tyler Herro and small forward Keldon Johnson, who declared early for the NBA draft, where they were all first round selections, there was some concern

But John Calipari rarely rebuilds. He just reloads as we saw again when the Wildcats (25-6, 15-3) caught fire midway through the season to win a 49th SEC regular season championship.

The Cats had a solid nucleus returning with sophomore forward EJ Montgomery, junior center Nick Richards and sophomore guards Aston Hagans and Immanuel Quickley. And Calipari added four talented freshmen, including two McDonald's All-Americans—forward Khalil Whitney and guard Tyrese Maxey—along with a 6'10" graduate transfer Nick Sestina, an all-Patriot League second team player from Bucknell.

Kentucky was ranked second in the AP preseason poll and started the season with a 69-62 over Michigan State in the Championships Classic in Madison Square Garden. Maxey was the star of stars with 26 as the Wildcats beat the preseason No. 1.

*University of Kentucky*

*Tyrese Maxey scored 27 points in a win over Louisville.*

University of Kentucky

*Immanuel Quickley was
SEC Player of the Year.*

But a week later, Kentucky looked far from invincible, losing at home to Evansville, 67-63, at the buzzer at Rupp. This was the biggest upset of the year and the worst loss at UK in the Calipari era, given the fact Evansville was 0-18 in the Missouri Valley Conference the prior season. Walter McCarty, who played for Kentucky under Rick Pitino, and his Aces came back to the Blue Grass and limited the poor shooting Cats to just 4-for-17 23.5 percent) from three-point range in an embarrassing loss.

In December, more bumps in the road. Kentucky lost back-to-back games to Utah and Ohio State in Las Vegas, leaving the team at 8-3. Kentucky began its turnaround when Maxey showed his love for big games by scoring 27 points in a 78-70 overtime victory against bitter in-state rival Louisville, igniting the spark that lifted the Cats to 17 wins in their final 20 games, including a 13-2 mark after switching to a three-guard lineup in a win at Arkansas Jan. 18.

The two biggest impact players during the surge were Quickley and Richards, who personally quieted the skeptics.

Quickley, a 6'3" McDonald's All-American guard from John Carroll in Havre de Grace, Md., made the unprecedented jump, going from 5.2 points and averaging 18.5 minutes as a freshman benchwarmer to college basketball superstar overnight. His development was one of the most rapid cases of anyone in the John Calipari era. Quickley's game took off at the start of conference season.

He averaged 18.4 points while shooting 47.8 percent from three-point range and 92 percent from the line in SEC games, and had 20 straight games scoring in double figures. He was named SEC Player of the Year by the league coaches and was joined on the coaches' All-SEC first team by Richards, who easily could have won the award himself.

University of Kentucky

*Nick Richards averaged
14 ppg. and 7.8 rpg.*

"One of my preseason goals was to make first team, but to win SEC Player of the Year, I don't think a lot of people thought I would be able to do something like this," Quickley said. "That's what makes it really cool, just to kind of be an underdog and come there and do something special."

The 6'11", 247-pound Richards, who was born in Jamaica and attended the Patrick School in Hillside, N.J., was also a McDonald's All-American. He evolved into one of the country's most consistent players throughout much of the season, averaging 14 points, 7.8 rebounds, and 2.1 blocks while shooting 64.2 percent after averaging just 3.9 points and 3.3 rebounds as a sophomore. Richards stepped up when Whitney did not live up to expectations and left the team in February.

He helped put the finishing touches on the Cats' fourth SEC regular season championship in six years when he scored 17 of his 19 points in the second half, leading the way as the sixth-ranked Cats rallied from an 18-point deficit to edge Florida. They did that without Hagans (who had been suspended after a loss to Tennessee the previous game), and also without Quickley (who fouled out with nine minutes to play) on the court and stunned the Gators, 71-70, in Gainesville in the final game of the regular season.

The SEC coaches named Calipari SEC Coach of the Year for a fourth time. Richards and Hagans were both voted to the All SEC defensive team and Maxey was named to first team All-Freshman team and second team All SEC.

This was the type of dangerous team that excelled on defense, holding opponents to 66 points and 39 percent shooting. They could have four players—Maxey, Quickley, Hagans and Richards—drafted if they declare. The Cats were playing some of the best—and most consistent—basketball in the country and had a shot to make a deep run into the tournament.

*University of Kentucky*

*John Calipari led the young Wildcats to a 25-win season.*

"How this team came together and the vibe that this team had, I felt this was a vibe that my best teams have had," Calipari said. "Our energy, our vibe, their togetherness. I looked at my staff and said, 'Guys we could be winning this whole thing.'"

# CHAPTER TEN

# THE BIG TEN DOMINANCE
## The Best There Was

The Big Ten has not won a national championship since Michigan State defeated Florida in the 2000 NCAA tournament title game and this monster all-sports conference has been looking for that elusive prize ever since.

But there is little question the Big Ten was clearly the strongest, deepest conference in the nation. The league was so competitive. Night in and night out, there were so many Maalox Mashers, and a number went overtime.

Maryland, Wisconsin, and Michigan State tied for a share of first place in the regular season with 14-6 records, one game ahead of Illinois. Everybody was looking forward to the sold-out conference tournament in Indianapolis to show off the product.

"If the regular season is any indication, the Big Ten tournament is going to be phenomenal for the fans, maybe a little stressful for the coaches," said Wisconsin coach Greg Gard, whose team won its final eight games to win a share of its first Big Ten title since 2014, when Bo Ryan was still in Madison.

The Big Ten boasted its share of great players. Junior center Luka Garza of Iowa was the Big Ten Player of the Year and was my national Player of the Year. Senior Cassius Winston of Michigan State was also an All-American and one of the premier leaders in college basketball. Senior guard Anthony Cowan and 6'9" sophomore All-America

*Brad Underwood had Illinois ready for its first NCAA trip since 2013.*

Mark Jones/Illinois Athletics

University of Iowa Athletic Communications

*Trayce Jackson-Davis, the son of former NBA star Dale Davis, led the Hoosiers in scoring (13.5 ppg.).*

forward Jalen Smith were standouts at Maryland. Sophomore center Daniel Oturu, another All-American, was a stud at Minnesota. Senior forward Lamar Stevens had a big year at Penn State. Sophomore guard Ayo Dosunmu led Illinois back to the big dance. Senior point guard Zavier Simpson dished Michigan to success in Juan Howard's first year.

The one thing I really liked about the Big Ten is they have strong bench coaching, top to bottom, and most of their stars stay around for more years and develop into better players. Most All-Big Ten players are upperclassmen. Only two Big Ten players—freshman guard Romeo Langford of Indiana and sophomore guard Jordan Poole of Michigan—had their names called in the first round of the 2019 NBA draft.

Six teams—Michigan State, Maryland, Wisconsin, Ohio State, Illinois, and Iowa—were ranked in the final AP Top 25, and 12 of the 14 teams were ranked in the top 42 of the NCAA's NET rankings. Nine teams were ranked in the Top 30 of KenPom.com. The Big Ten won the Gavitt Games, 5-3, against select Big East competition, and the Big Ten-ACC challenge, 8-6, including Purdue's 69-40 victory over defending national champion Virginia.

Last year, the Big Ten had eight teams invited to the dance and all but one advanced and picked up at least one win. Michigan State defeated Duke in the Elite Eight to advance to its eighth Final Four.

This year, I had 10—Wisconsin (21-10), Maryland (24-7), Michigan State (22-9), Illinois (21-10), Iowa (21-10), Ohio State (21-10), Penn State (21-10), Rutgers (20-11), Michigan (19-12), and Indiana (20-12)—one short of the 11 the Big East sent in 2011—penciled into my Vitale NCAA bracket.

MSU Athletics Communications

*Xavier Tillman was the Big Ten Defensive Player of the Year.*

Maryland coach Mark Turgeon called it "the best conference I've coached in, top to bottom."

"It was an unprecedented league this season," Indiana coach Archie Miller said. "It was from the start of the season to the final day, the best league in America, the deepest league in America."

Minnesota coach Richard Pitino said he saw a list of the teams in the country with the toughest strength of schedule and said a dozen Big Ten teams were in the top 15. "We're sitting at eight wins in the league and, in a normal year, we might be at 11 or 12," he said. "That's just how tough this league has been."

The Big Ten was wildly unpredictable and any team could win on a given night. "It's been the most difficult season in my 25 years," Michigan State coach Tom Izzo admitted.

Unlike any conference in the country, numerous ranked teams were at the bottom of standings, probably because the league had 38 wins over ranked opponents.

Consider Michigan. The Wolverines were 10-10 in league play and finished ninth in conference play but they still had enough in the tank to beat then No. 6 North Carolina, and then No. 8 Gonzaga, 82-64, in the Battle4Atlantis in the Bahamas loaded eight-team tournament I did for ESPN in November.

*Michigan Photography*

*Zavier Simpson led the Big Ten in assists (7.9 apg.)*

*Kelsea Garthoff/Illinois Athletics*

*Ayo Dosunmu led Illinois to its best record in a decade.*

Purdue was at 16-15 and 9-11 in the league, but the Boilermakers still defeated Virginia, 69-40, in the Big Ten-ACC Challenge at West Lafayette.

With one or two exceptions, most of the marquee non-league matchups weren't close. Ohio State defeated Villanova, 76-51, at Columbus, and Kentucky, 71-52, in Vegas. Indiana defeated Florida State, 84-60, in the ACC-Big Ten Challenge at Bloomington. Maryland beat up Notre Dame, 72-51 and Marquette, 84-63, at College Park. Penn State defeated Syracuse, 85-64, in State College. Iowa defeated Texas Tech, 72-61, in Vegas, Wisconsin defeated Tennessee, 68-48, in Knoxville, and Michigan State beat Seton Hall, 76-73, in Newark.

The Big Ten league games were Battle Royals. Think about these games:

WISCONSIN OVER Ohio State, 61-57.

Wisconsin's Nate Reuvers' jumper finally wrested the lead away from Ohio State, with 1:54 left in the game, and the Wisconsin forward hit four free throws in the last 14 seconds to seal a road upset of the No. 5 Buckeyes.

WISCONSIN OVER Maryland, 56-54

Brad Davison hit a 3-pointer with 11 seconds left after getting a steal, and Wisconsin beat No. 17 Maryland.

WISCONSIN OVER Michigan State, 64-63

Wisconsin earned the win despite missing both Brad Davison and Kobe King.

WISCONSIN OVER Purdue, 69-65

Aleem Ford scored a career-high 19 points, and the Badgers hit eight straight free throws with less than 30 seconds left.

WISCONSIN OVER Minnesota, 71-69

Brad Davison scored 20 points as Wisconsin rallied from a late deficit to beat Minnesota. The Golden Gophers' inability to make free throws late hurt.

WISCONSIN OVER Indiana, 60-56

The Hoosiers led 51-44 at the 6:52 mark.

MARYLAND OVER Illinois, 59-58

Anthony Cowan Jr. hit a tying 3-pointer in the final 20 seconds and a go-ahead free throw with 2.1 seconds left, as Maryland rallied from a 15-point deficit.

ILLINOIS OVER Michigan, 64-62

Ayo Dosunmu took advantage of his five-inch-height-edge on Zavier Simpson, sinking a contested jumper from the free throw line with 0.5 seconds left on the clock.

MINNESOTA OVER Ohio State, 62-59

Marcus Carr's 3-pointer with three seconds left in the game secured the win.

MARYLAND OVER Indiana, 77-76

Jalen Smith came up big, converting on a pass from Anthony Cowan Jr. in the post; the sophomore forward scored on a layup with 14.5 seconds left to cap an improbable last-minute comeback for the Terps. Maryland scored the final seven points.

MARYLAND OVER Nebraska, 72-70

Expect the unexpected. No easy games in the Big Ten. The Terrapins blew most of a 14-point lead against lowly Nebraska before escaping with a 72-70 victory.

ILLINOIS OVER Wisconsin, 71-70

Kobe King of the Badgers drained a 3 with 22 seconds left to pull Wisconsin to within 71-70, but when the Badgers got the ball back after a missed free throw by Illinois, D'Mitrik Trice missed a go-ahead bucket with three seconds left.

MARYLAND OVER Minnesota, 74-73

Down by double digits for most of the game and trailing by eight points near the two-minute mark, Maryland could've chalked up an off night at Minnesota to the rigor of Big Ten road play. Darryl Morsell drained the go-ahead 3-pointer with 1.9 seconds left, capping a furious comeback for a 74-73 victory with a 10-1 run over the final 2:06.

INDIANA OVER Michigan State, 67-63

Joey Brunk scored 14 points including a layup with one minute to go.

PENN STATE OVER Rutgers, 65-64

Myles Dread hit a go-ahead 3-pointer with 28 seconds left to lift Penn State.

ILLINOIS OVER Indiana, 67-66

Ayo Dosunmu hit a key three-pointer with 1:28 left to put Illinois up 65-60.

MARYLAND OVER Rutgers, 56-51

Anthony Cowan made three free throws to put the Terrapins up 52-49 with 2:12 to go.

PENN STATE OVER Iowa, 89-86

Izaiah Brockington scored 23 points, and Mike Watkins' fast-break dunk with 1:42 left, put No. 21 Penn State ahead to stay, at the Palestra.

ILLINOIS OVER Northwestern, 75-71

Illinois led 69-60 with 3:50 remaining and hung on.

OHIO STATE OVER Michigan, 61-58

Kyle Young made two free throws with 33.3 seconds remaining to give Ohio State the lead after a crucial replay review.

PENN STATE OVER Michigan State, 75-70

Lamar Stevens had 24 points, leading the 22nd-ranked Nittany Lions to a 75-70 win over No. 16 Michigan State. Cassius Winston scored 25 points, but could not convert on two chances to pull into a tie in the closing seconds.

MICHIGAN STATE OVER Illinois, 70-69

Plenty of drama in the closing seconds. Star guard Ayo Dosunmu crumbled to the floor, clutching his left knee moments after Michigan State's Xavier Tillman threw down a huge dunk that lifted the Spartans to the win.

PURDUE OVER Minnesota, 83-78 IN 2 OT

Matt Haarms scored 26 points in the thriller.

IOWA OVER Rutgers, 85-80

Luka Garza had 28 points and 13 rebounds.

MICHIGAN OVER Purdue, 84-78, IN 2 OT

Zavier Simpson scored 22 points and made big shots late.

ILLINOIS OVER Rutgers, 54-51

Ayo Dosunmu stepped up big in the final two minutes for Illinois as he scored four points (all at the free-throw line) to seal a defensive battle.

ILLINOIS OVER Iowa, 78-76

Luka Garza scored 28 points, but it was not enough.

IOWA OVER Minnesota, 58-55

Luka Garza had 24 points and the Hawkeyes closed the game by scoring the final 11 points.

RUTGERS OVER Purdue, 71-68 IN OT

Geo Baker scored 19 points, including a crucial late basket, to help lift Rutgers to an overtime victory.

NEBRASKA OVER Iowa, 76-70

Thorir Thorbjarnarson hit a pair of 3-pointers in a 10-3 Nebraska spurt that put the Huskers up 69-62, paving the way to the winning score.

RUTGERS OVER Nebraska, 75-72

Geo Baker hit a 3 with 1.2 seconds left to send No. 24 Rutgers past Nebraska.

RUTGERS OVER Northwestern, 77-73 IN OT

Geo Baker had 25 points, six rebounds, and five assists as Rutgers overcame an 18-point deficit.

PURDUE OVER Northwestern, 61-58

Sasha Stefanovic made a 3-pointer with 3.1 seconds left.

INDIANA OVER Nebraska, 96-90 IN OT

Rob Phinisee scored seven of his season-high 16 points at the start of overtime.

INDIANA OVER Northwestern, 66-62

Trayce Jackson-Davis made the tie-breaking free throws with 1:57 left, then punctuated the late comeback with an alley-oop dunk to help Indiana close out a win.

INDIANA OVER Minnesota, 72-67

Trayce Jackson-Davis finished with 18 points and nine rebounds in 31 minutes.

NORTHWESTERN OVER Nebraska, 62-57

Miller Kopp scored 15 points and Northwestern snapped a five-game losing streak.

NORTHWESTERN OVER Nebraska, 81-76 IN OT

Miller Kopp took Northwestern's first shot in overtime, draining a three-pointer that triggered a 7-0 Wildcat run.

It was a special season for the Big Ten. We will never know if they would have gained that first national championship since 2000.

# CHAPTER ELEVEN

# BIG EAST DEPTH

## Deep Six in Dance

Villanova coach Jay Wright is generally considered one of the best coaches in college basketball and a future Naismith Hall-of-Famer. He was recently selected as the AP Coach of the Decade after winning six of seven regular season championships and four tournament championships after the Big East re-organized into a 10-team basketball-centric league in the 2013-2014 season. He won two national championships in 2016 and 2018.

"We look at the league as a really unique entity in college athletics," Wright said. "Every place we play is a passionate basketball place with great tradition. Almost every team has been to a Final Four. We like being part of it. All the decisions the athletic directors made focus on basketball."

But this past year, the 10th-ranked Wildcats (24-7) had to share the wealth with 15th-ranked Seton Hall (21-9) and 7th-ranked Creighton (24-7), who each grabbed a share of the Big East regular season title with 13-5 records, showing the rest of the country this fluid league is more than one elite team. Eight teams won at least 18 games and four—including 23rd-ranked Butler (22-9)— won more than 20.

This was a year when six teams—Villanova, Creighton, the Hall, Butler, Providence, and Marquette—figured to receive bids to the Big Dance, and the league produced two first team All-Americans—senior guards Myles Powell of the Hall and Markus Howard of Marquette.

*Allen Kee / ESPN Images*

*Jay Wright was*
*AP Coach of the Decade.*

*Jeremiah Robinson-Earl was Villanova's Freshman of the Year.*

It was a lot better than 2019 when the proud Big East had just four bids to the tournament—Villanova, Seton Hall, Marquette, and St. John's—and none of them made it to the Sweet 16, a major disappointment. The Red Storm, which was considered the last team to make the 68-team field, lost to Arizona State in a First Four game at Dayton.

The nightmare continued when Marquette was upset in the first round by Murray State when Racers' 6'3" sophomore point guard Ja Morant, the Ohio Valley Player of the Year and the second pick overall in the NBA draft, went off for 17 points, 11 rebounds, and 16 assists in an 83-64 win over the fifth-seeded Eagles in a game. He outplayed Howard in Hartford, Conn. The same night, Fletcher Magee set the Division I career record for three-pointers and poured in 24 points, as seventh-seeded Wofford rolled to an 84-68 victory over 10th-seeded Seton Hall in Jacksonville.

Villanova, the defending national champion, couldn't even get out of the first weekend, losing to Carsen Edwards and Purdue by 26 points. Edwards was Awesome, Baby, with a Capital A! He made nine threes and scored 42 points in the second-seeded Boilermakers' 87-61 victory over the sixth-seeded Cats at Hartford.

Villanova was out and no Big East teams were in the Sweet 16. This was a league that once set a record for most teams invited to the tournament with 11 in 2011, the same year original member, Connecticut, won the national championship.

Going into this season, there was an expectation the Big East would have more than four teams in the bracket. Yet preseason polls showed limited belief in Creighton and Butler. The Bluejays were projected as the seventh best team in the league in the coaches' preseason poll. Butler was picked eighth.

Seton Hall was a slight favorite over Villanova to capture the conference crown.

The Big East was extremely competitive during the regular season. DePaul, picked last in the preseason poll, was an early surprise at 12-1 with impressive non-league wins over Iowa, Minnesota, Boston College, and Texas Tech. The Blue Demons only won three games in league play, but were competitive enough to defeat Butler and Marquette and take Villanova to overtime on the Main Line.

The race for the regular season championship came down to the last day. Sophomore guard Marcus Zegarowski made all five of his three-pointers and finished with 23 points as the Bluejays, which lost two projected starters prior to the season, defeated Seton Hall, 77-60, before a sellout crowd of 18,000 in Omaha. They claimed all or part of their first conference title since winning the Missouri Valley outright in 2012-2013.

They joined the Big East the next season. Creighton, Seton Hall, and Villanova all finished with the same record, one game ahead of a Providence team that came on strong with six straight wins. The Bluejays won 11 of their last 13 games and, because they swept the season series against the Pirates and defeated Villanova in Philadelphia, they earned the No. 1 seed in the Big East tournament at the Garden.

"Did we think it was possible? We knew it was going to be hard. Did we know the league was going to be this good? Probably not at that time," Big East Coach of the Year Doug McDermott said. "So, to be sitting in this situation is incredible. When a group of people come together and they believe in each other, and when they don't care who gets the credit, there are a lot of things that are possible."

McDermott's team was led by junior guard Ty-Shon Alexander, an All-Big East selection who averaged 16.9 points; and Zegarowski, who averaged 16.1 points. Zegarowski injured his knee at the end of the win over the Hall and missed the Big East quarterfinal game against St. John's, which lasted a half before the NCAA canceled all conference tournament games because of a growing coronavirus outbreak that has since ravaged New York City. Creighton's depth was impressive. Six players averaged at least 8.6 points.

Seton Hall led the conference race much of the season, but went 3-4 in its last seven games, including consecutive losses to Villanova at home and Creighton, to end the regular season. Powell impressed the coaches enough to beat out Howard for Big East Player of the Year, averaging 21 points and 4.3 rebounds.

Wright led a young Villanova team, which did not have a senior in its six-man rotation, to its seventh straight season with at least 24 wins. The Cats would have added to that total with Big East and NCAA tourney wins for sure. They might have reached 30 wins for the fifth time in seven years.

*Myles Powell earned Big East Player of the Year honors.*

Seton Hall Athletics

The Cats had several scoring threats, with five players averaging double figures. Sophomore 6'8" forward Saddiq Bey, who was a first team All-Big East selection and won the Julius Erving Award as the best small forward in the country, was the team leader at 16.1 points per game. He led the conference in three-point shooting, making 48.4 percent of his shots from beyond the arc, followed by junior point guard Collin Gillespie, a second team selection, at 15.1 points. Jeremiah Robinson-Earl, a 6'9" former McDonald's All-American, was an easy choice for Big East Freshman of the Year on a team that was picked preseason No. 1 in ESPN's spring Top 25 for 2021.

Ed Cooley's Providence Friars were a remarkable comeback story. PC was 6-6 through 12 games, including losses to College of Charleston, Northwestern, Rhode Island, Long Beach State and Penn. The Friars six straight Big East wins to end the campaign tied the team's longest winning streak in league play, last accomplished in 2017. Providence earned 12 Big East wins for the first time in school history, finishing 12-6 in league play.

For the first time in the history of the program, the Friars defeated every team in the Big East at least once during the regular season. Providence posted a 5-4 record versus ranked teams. That included a big win at Villanova. Senior 6'7" guard Alpha Diallo, a second team All-Big East selection, averaged 14.1 points and 7.8 rebounds in 31 games. He posted a double-double in nine of those games, including a 35-point, 10-rebound performance versus Seton Hall on February 15.

*Marquette Athletics*

*Markus Howard led the NCAA in scoring.*

Marquette was led by Howard, who led the nation in scoring with 27.8 points a game and set a conference career scoring record with 1,587 points. The Golden Eagles started 10-2, with wins over USC and Purdue. Unfortunately, they closed 1-6 in their last seven games to finish 8-10 in league play. But their resumé was strong enough to dance despite the late slide.

Butler started off as a major surprise, winning 15 of its first 16 games. The Bulldogs built a strong resumé with non-league wins over Florida, Stanford, Purdue, Minnesota, Ole Miss, and Missouri. Then, the bottom dropped out and Butler went 4-8 in a 12-game span before closing the season with three straight wins. Senior guard Kamar Baldwin, who averaged 16.2 points and 3.3 assists, made 85 percent of his free throws, and had a 36-point outburst in a win over Xavier in the season finale, made first team All-Big East.

The Big East had 60 percent of its teams projected to dance. The Big Ten, generally considered the best conference in the country, was looking at placing 10 of 15 teams in the bracket. Both of these conferences had a lot to be proud of as March Madness approached.

The Big East had seven players average at least 16 points in 2019-20:

| | |
|---|---|
| Markus Howard, Marquette | 27.8 |
| Myles Powell, Seton Hall | 21.0 |
| Ty-Shon Alexander, Creighton | 16.9 |
| Naji Marshall, Xavier | 16.8 |
| Kamar Baldwin, Butler | 16.2 |
| Marcus Zegarowski, Creighton | 16.1 |
| Saddiq Bey, Villanova | 16.1 |

# CHAPTER TWELVE

# LUKA GARZA IS LUKA STARZA

The envelope please.

My personal choice for the National Player of the Year for the 2019-2020 season, checking with my Dick Vitale Bald Dome Index, was 6'11", 260-pound junior forward, Luka Garza, of Iowa. It wasn't an easy decision. I had Big East Player of the Year Myles Powell of Seton Hall high on my list early in the season, but eventually the choice came down to Garza and 6'9" redshirt sophomore Obi Toppin of Dayton. Garza and Toppin. It was a very tough decision. I tossed and turned for several nights, but in the end, I went with Garza. He averaged 23.9 points and 9.8 rebounds for the Hawkeyes, was an AP first-team All-America, had 25 20-point games, and 15 double doubles against big-time competition. That was the difference for me. It's not that Toppin couldn't do it.

Toppin, who declared for the draft, will be a lottery pick. Garza is not up on the NBA draft charts. He's not a Top 5 draft pick, but he decided to test the waters. I have a feeling he may come back for his senior year. I talked to his coach Fran McCaffery and he told me he never had a kid with the work ethic or the desire that Garza brought.

*University of Iowa Athletic Communications*

*Garza was the Big Ten Men's Basketball Player of the Year.*

He played hard, with a lot of feeling.

Six other outlets have already named Garza National Player of the Year: *Sporting News, Basketball Times, The Athletic, Stadium, Bleacher Report,* and *ESPN.* He is the first Iowa player to earn that kind of distinction. Garza also earned the Kareem Abdul-Jabbar award for best center in college basketball.

The Washington, D.C., native averaged 26.7 points, 11.1 rebounds, and 1.7 blocks in 12 games against AP-ranked opponents. He is the only Big Ten player to register seven 25-point, 10-rebound performances in the same season in more than 17 years. He produced the two highest point totals in a game by a Big Ten player (44 at Michigan and 38 at Indiana).

Garza had a dream season.

It was his way of trying to live up to his blood lines. The Garza family is from Bosnia and Herzegovina. Dad, Frank Garza, was a 6'7" forward at Idaho in the mid-1980s, when the three-point shot was introduced to the college game. Garza's mother, Sejla, competed professionally in Europe. Garza has a grandfather who played at Hawaii; his uncle, Teoman Alibegovic, played for Oregon State and was the Slovenian national team's all-time leading scorer; and his cousin, Amar Alibegovic, played for St. John's.

*University of Iowa Athletic Communications*

*Garza was named Naismith Kareem Abdul-Jabbar Center of the Year.*

When Garza was young, he used to watch videotapes that his father collected of former NBA post players like Kareem Abdul-Jabbar and he attempted to recreate their moves. "Other people were watching Nickelodeon," Garza recalled. "I was downstairs watching the (video) cassette tapes of these guys…I had a bunch of them in the old TV and I was just sitting down there and I'd get the little mini-basketball and try to recreate their moves."

Garza enrolled at the Maret School in Washington, D.C., where he played for Chuck Driesell, the son of renowned Hall-of-Fame coach Lefty Driesell, who had just taken over the program. Driesell got his first look at Garza the summer after his sophomore year when he was playing for Team Takeover in an AAU tournament in Maryland. Driesell was impressed by Garza's skill set but was concerned his bulky frame might limit his ability to run the floor.

As it turns out, Garza, whose childhood nickname was "Pudge," was aware of his weight problem. He'd had surgery to repair bone spurs after his sophomore year and ballooned to 265 pounds during a period of inactivity. Garza spent August 2015 in Hawaii, working out with his father, Frank, and Frank's former college coach, Bill Trumbo. Garza went on a diet and added more sprints to his training regimen. He dropped 30 pounds and emerged as a big-time prospect who wound up with 28 offers. He chose Iowa over Georgetown and Notre Dame because of an early bond with McCaffery.

Garza led Maret to a 26-5 record as a senior when he averaged 24.6 points, 11.7 rebounds, and 2.5 blocks while shooting 69 percent and 48 percent from three-point range. He was selected as Gatorade Player of the Year in D.C. and he dominated the D.C. State Association tournament. Garza saved his best effort for his final game against national power Gonzaga in the city championship with his face up, back to the basket, versatility, and scoring ability. Garza did not get off to a good start in the first half of that game at George Washington U. He had a defender pinned on his back and rose for a shot.

*Garza set the Iowa Single-Season Scoring Record (740 points), and is one of three Big Ten players ever to amass 740+ points and 300+ rebounds in a season.*

University of Iowa Athletic Communications

When the defender tried to block his shot, he caught Garza with an elbow that sent him sprawling into some camera equipment. Garza's head was split open. There was blood everywhere and Garza needed stitches.

But he came back from a halftime cleanup to score 37 points and grabbed 17 rebounds during a 77-66 loss.

It took Garza a year to come into his own at Iowa. He was a double-figure scorer as a sophomore, anchoring the frontcourt with Tyler Cook. Garza became the face of the team this year after star guard Jordan Bohannon missed the season recovering from hip surgery.

He was selected Big Ten Player of the Year after scoring 20 or more points in the final 16 games as Iowa carved out a 20-11 record and locked up a spot in the tournament. He scored 25 points or more 13 times and had seven games with at least 25 points and 10 rebounds. His 26.2 points in conference games was the highest since Purdue's Glenn Robinson, who averaged 31.1 points in 1994.

# CHAPTER THIRTEEN

# AUBURN AND BRUCE PEARL

## From the Final Four to…More Great Things

He is the only coach to take UW-Milwaukee to an NCAA Sweet 16 in 2005. He is the only coach to take Tennessee to a No. 1 ranking in 2008 and an NCAA Elite Eight in 2010. And he is the only coach to take Auburn to 30 wins, an NCAA Final Four in 2019 as a #5 seed, and the memories of wins over Kansas and North Carolina, and a 77-70 overtime victory against conference rival Kentucky in the Midwest Region finals.

Yes, Auburn made the Final Four in 2019.

Bruce Pearl, a one-time student manager under Dr. Tom Davis at Boston College, has been a successful head coach for 24 years. He keeps breaking new barriers on the Plains, transforming a traditional SEC football school into a national basketball power. The Tigers began last season's SEC season 2-4, with a three-game losing streak, but they battled back, won the SEC tournament, landed a #5 seed, and made a deep run in March.

By all accounts, after losing three elite starters in guards Jared Harper and Bryce Brown and forward Chuma Okeke, the Tigers should have taken a step back.

But the train kept rolling. The Tigers started 21-2, won 25 games and finished second to Kentucky in the SEC regular season with a 12-6 record. The Tigers used a combination of five solid seniors—guards Samir Doughty

*Auburn Athletics*

*Bruce Pearl has won 81 games over the last three seasons.*

81

Auburn Athletics

*Samir Doughty led Auburn in scoring (16.7 ppg.).*

and J'Von McCormick; 6'11", 260-pound center Austin Wiley; and forwards Danjel Purifoy and Anfernee McLemore—who were adjusting to new roles. They added a diaper dandy in 6'6" star Isaac Okoro, who should be a high lottery pick in the NBA draft, to keep the flame alive and play their way into the Big Dance for a third straight year.

This Auburn team was experienced. They knew growth was the name of the game. 'I've got five seniors," Pearl said. "They want to make their own history. That's not living off last year's team."

"I am extremely proud of this group for finishing in second place because the league was so good. I felt like this was a team that could finish in the Top 5. To finish higher than we were picked and be within range of the champion, I was very pleased."

The Tigers split with Kentucky, winning 75-66 at home when Doughty scored 23 points and made 14-of-15 free throws. Auburn lost 73-66 at Rupp when Cats' guard and SEC Player of the Year Immanuel Quickley scored 18 points and grabbed 12 rebounds.

Auburn made a habit of scaling seemingly insurmountable obstacles. The Tigers overcame a 17-point deficit against Tennessee with an 18-0 run on their way to a home win over the Vols. They climbed from a 19-point hole to beat Ole Miss in Oxford in double overtime. They erased LSU's 15-point lead to beat the Tigers in overtime. "These kids really cared," Pearl said. "They grinded. They won five overtime games. I'm proud of the way they competed, especially with a roster with a lot of seniors that played supporting cast roles the year before and played dominant roles."

Bruce is an unbelievable communicator. And he does it with passion. In 2007, Pearl attended a Lady Vols game with his upper body painted orange. He and a few of his players spelled out "V-O-L-S" and stood in front of the student section and cheered for the women's team as they came out. His actions brought national attention to the Tennessee program and highlighted efforts to support women's athletics. Later that season, Pat Summitt returned the favor on Senior Night. Before the game, Summitt came out as a cheerleader, complete with uniform, and she led the crowd in a rendition of "Rocky Top."

The seventh-largest crowd in school history also witnessed Pearl's team rout the then fourth-ranked and defending national champion Florida Gators.

Pearl really knows the game and he can really recruit, there's no doubt about that. But there have been times when it has gotten him in trouble. Pearl was hit with a five-year show-cause penalty from the NCAA after inviting a high school junior, Aaron Craft, and the members of his family, to a cookout at his Knoxville home while Craft was on an unofficial visit to UT. That was a violation of NCAA rules. When the NCAA began to investigate, Pearl not only lied about the cookout, but also told the father to lie as well. The end result: Pearl was eventually fired by the school and was not allowed to coach again until 2014.

But he came back stronger than ever in his six years at Auburn. This year was typical.

What would Auburn do without Harper and Brown? McCormick and Doughty answered that, forming one of the top guard combos in the SEC. Doughty, who lead Auburn in scoring at 16.7 points per game, put the finishing touches on his season, scoring 32 points and hitting a career-high eight three-pointers during the Tigers' 85-63 win at Tennessee. It was a high point for Doughty, the VCU transfer, who was a first team All-SEC selection.

How would the Tigers replace Okeke? It took a collective effort, but Purifoy and McLemore both stepped up and filled in admirably. A healthy Wiley also proved just how dominant he could be, finishing second in the SEC in rebounding.

*Pearl in the huddle.*

Auburn Athletics

Wiley arrived at Auburn with immense promise and a great pedigree as the son of two former Auburn greats, three-time All-American and Olympian Vickie Orr Wiley and Aubrey Wiley, who led the SEC in rebounding in 1994. He immediately showed his potential after enrolling midyear as a freshman and averaging 8.8 points and 4.7 rebounds in 23 games. He lost his sophomore season after being embroiled in college basketball's FBI scandal and returned as a junior in a reserve role for the Tigers' Final Four team.

*Auburn Athletics*

*Isaac Okoro averaged 12.9 ppg. while shooting 51.4 percent from the floor.*

This year, Wiley reinvented himself. He averaged a career-best 10.6 points and 9.3 rebounds and shot a career best 67.1 percent from the free throw line after entering his senior year as a career 52.5 percent shooter.

Okoro was an added plus, the best of Pearl's five freshman recruits. He averaged 12.9 points, 4.4 rebounds and two assists per game while being named to the SEC All-Defensive, SEC All-Freshman and second team All-SEC teams. Okoro excelled as Auburn's top defender, often drawing the matchup with an opponent's best player throughout the year, and has decided to declare for the draft and go through the evaluation process.

It was never going to be easy to follow the team that made the first Final Four appearance in school history, but this team left their mark on Auburn basketball.

Auburn has won almost as many games over the last three years as they did in the prior six:

Last 3 years: 81-24

Prior 6 years: 82-109

The past three seasons have been among the best in Auburn history:

| Year | Wins |
| --- | --- |
| 2018-19 | 30 |
| 1998-99 | 29 |
| 2017-18 | 26 |
| 2019-20 | 25 |

## CHAPTER FOURTEEN

# NATIONAL CHAMPION VIRGINIA TRIES TO DEFEND

The University of Virginia has been a great college basketball story over the last three seasons. The Cavaliers, who won their first national championship in 2019 and have become perennial contenders for the ACC title, have had to fight some unexpected adversity throughout this golden era. But Cavaliers' coach Tony Bennett is constantly figuring out a way to overcome the obstacles.

Virginia dominated the ACC regular season in 2018 and emerged as a national contender after putting up a 33-3 record, including 17-1 in conference play. The Cavaliers won both the regular season and ACC tournament. Their overwhelming success earned them a No. 1 seed in the NCAA South Region and a supposedly easy matchup against 16th-seeded Maryland-Baltimore County from the America East Conference.

Then, the day we all thought would never come to March Madness finally arrived. After 135 tries, Ryan Odom's UMBC Retrievers became the first 16th-seed to dispose of a No. 1 since the tournament expanded to 64 teams in 1985, defeating Virginia, 74-54, in Charlotte. Many called it the biggest upset in tournament history. UMBC was listed as a 5,000-to-1 shot in Vegas. Virginia was the clear favorite to win the South Region at 6-to-5. But senior guard Jairus Lyles, who made a game-winning 25-foot jumper at

*Tony Bennett is 89-13 over the last three years.*

*Mamadi Diakite scored in double figures
in 26 of 30 games this season.*

the buzzer to beat heavy favorite Vermont in the America East championship game, put on another dazzling display to destroy Virginia's pack-line defense. Lyles became a campus legend when he scored with 28 points on 9-of-11 shooting and played much of the second half fighting cramps. Bennett handled the loss with class. He gave Ryan Odom and UMBC their just due.

The next year, Bennett was rewarded for his classy outlook. The Cavaliers completed the ultimate act of redemption when they defeated Texas Tech, 85-77 in overtime at the NCAA championship game in Minneapolis. Kyle Guy was named Most Outstanding Player after scoring 24 points to go with his game-winning three free throws to defeat Auburn in the semi-finals.

Sophomore guard De'Andre Hunter, who missed the 2018 blowout loss to UMBC because of an injury, practically carried the Cavaliers to their first national title with 27 points and nine rebounds. His baseline three-pointer with 12 seconds left in regulation tied the score, forced overtime, and set up a game deciding 11-0 run.

"It's unbelievable," Hunter said after the Cavs became the only team to win a title the year after losing in the first round. "Especially with what happened last year and losing in the first round. We talked about this all season and what happened."

Guy, Hunter, and guard Ty Jerome all shined and all three heard their names called in the NBA draft, with Hunter emerging as the fourth pick overall to Atlanta. Without Guy, Hunter, and Jerome, the Cavaliers still had major expectations. Guard Kihei Clark, wing forward Braxton Key, forward Mamadi Diakite, and 7'0" center Jay Huff were all experienced players and Virginia was picked 11th in the AP preseason poll.

*Kihei Clark led Virginia with 177 assists.*

Bennett's team lacked the three-point shooters it had the year before, but it still displayed its trademark tenacious defense when the season started, holding Syracuse to 34 points on 59 possessions in a 48-34 victory and then limiting James Madison to 34 points on 69 trips in a 65-34 victory. The Cavaliers started the season 7-0.

Then Virginia hit the skids. First came a 69-40 loss to an inconsistent Purdue team. The Cavs went 5-6 in an 11-game span, including losses to South Carolina and Boston College. The talent drain forced them to go back to their roots and win the hard way in low-scoring games, using a glacial pace and suffocating defense. Sitting at 12-6 overall, Bennett saw his team go on a major roll, winning 11-of-12 games and eight straight to the end of the regular season. The lone loss in that stretch came at Louisville. Virginia's run included victories over Duke, Florida State, and Louisville by a combined 10 points.

*Diakite led the Cavaliers in scoring (13.7 ppg.).*

"A lot of people might say we're not the prettiest team," Bennett said. "We don't always play beautiful. We can be awkward at times. At times, it can be painful. But I say, 'Embrace it. Just play the heck out of the defense and get better—and don't try being something you are not.'"

Virginia had 16 games decided by single digits and three that went into overtime, but that put them in position to upset Duke and Florida State. They were 10-2 in games decided by five points or less and all but locked up another NCAA bid when they held Duke, the nation's third leading scoring team (82.3) to just 50 points in a 52-50 victory at the John Paul Jones Arena in Charlottesville, Virginia.

Huff, playing his best game of the year, had 10 blocks and iced the game by stuffing Devils' 6'10" Vernon Carey Jr.'s layup that would have given Duke the lead.

After the game, Bennett was asked how his blood pressure was. "Where it is always," he said. "All year. Every game. It's high."

Tony has a system and they play to that system, and the one thing they do is play a lot of 50-point games. So they're going to hang with you and hang with you. And they are so acclimated to playing those sorts of games. You look at those eight wins: 53-51, 55-53. You post those games and every one of them is right down to the wire. In fact, I was with Mike Krzyzewski before Duke played them and he was very specific with me. He said, "We got to end this one. We got to be in command with three or four minutes to go and, if it's going down to one or two points with a minute to go, my kids have not been in that situation."

Virginia lives for that scenario. They succeed at that. They feel like that is their winning time. And they have the mental ability to believe they are going to make that play. And sure enough, against Duke, it came right down to a last possession.

The Cavaliers (23-7) finished in a three-way tie for second in the ACC standings with a 15-5 record, just one game behind Florida State. Virginia, to no one's surprise, led the nation in scoring defense (52.4 points), second in field goal defense (36.9 percent, trailing only Memphis) and second in fouls per game (13.2, behind Notre Dame).

It all comes down to the leader. He lost a lot of guys—including three of them to the NBA—and, to come back and be that good, was really impressive.

The Cavaliers led the nation in scoring defense for the fourth straight season:

| YEAR | PPG. ALLOWED | NATIONAL RANK |
| --- | --- | --- |
| 2015-16 | 60.1 | 2nd |
| 2016-17 | 56.4 | 1st |
| 2017-18 | 54.0 | 1st |
| 2018-19 | 56.1 | 1st |
| 2019-20 | 52.4 | 1st |

# CHAPTER FIFTEEN

# PAC-12 BOUNCES BACK

The Pac-12 disappeared off the NCAA Tournament radar in 2018 and 2019. Just three teams—Washington, Oregon, and Arizona State—from that conference earned received invites to the big dance in 2018. And, in 2019, only three more—Arizona, Arizona State, and UCLA—went dancing, with ASU playing in the First Four.

This season, the West Coast flexed its muscles, baby, and it wasn't just Gonzaga and San Diego State. Based on the way the Pac-12 improved in 2020, the conference figured to rebound in March with an influx of more squads. My VBDI (Vitale Bald Dome Index) had six teams—Oregon, Arizona, Arizona State, USC, Colorado, and UCLA—in the field.

It was a big year, especially in Westwood, where the UCLA Bruins got in as one of my last four. Mick Cronin's team made quite a run to gain a berth. UCLA (19-12) was 8-9, with losses to Cal State-Fullerton, Hofstra, and Washington State. Some questioned if the Bruins, who offered and were rejected by big names like John Calipari and Jay Wright, had made the right decision when they plucked Cronin, a traditional, slow tempo, defensive-oriented coach, out of Cincinnati.

Then came a major turnaround as the Bruins challenged for the Pac-12 regular season title, falling one game short. A 54-52 loss to crosstown rival USC in the regular season finale was costly.

*Cronin saw UCLA go 11-3 in its final 14 games.*

Still, the Bruins went 11-3 in their last 14 games and won seven of their last eight after losing their top three scorers. They were good enough to play their way into the brackets after missing out in 2019. Cronin earned Pac-12 Coach of the Year honors after taking one of his teams to the tournament for the 13th time in 14 years. Chris Smith, a bouncy 6'9" junior guard with a versatile skill set, was named the Pac-12's Most Improved Player and was a first team All-Pac 12 selection after averaging 13.1 points, 5.4 rebounds, and 1.6 assists, with a career high 30 points in a win over Colorado.

*Oregon Athletic Communications*

*Pritchard averaged 20.5 ppg. and 5.5 apg.*

Oregon was a Top 20 team for most of the season, finishing 13th in the AP poll. Senior guard Payton Pritchard was the star of stars, averaging 20.5 points, four rebounds and 5.4 assists, and making big plays in crunch time for the 24-7 Ducks, who won their third regular season title in five years. Pritchard scored 29 points as Oregon defeated Stanford, 80-67, in the final game of the schedule to win the regular season title outright with a 13-5 record.

Pritchard, who has been part of four NCAA tournament teams, including a trip to the Final Four in 2017, was the unanimous choice as conference Player of the Year. Dana Altman felt he had the talent to make another deep run again.

Arizona, led by a trio of freshmen, came back from a disappointing 17-15 season and produced under Sean Miller. Guards Nico Mannion and Josh Green were heralded diaper dandies who were McDonald's All-Americans that lived up to expectations. Big man Zeke Nnaji made the biggest surprise. Nnaji arrived at Arizona with less hype than the stellar backcourt. But the 6'11" forward's NBA draft stock quickly rose as he dominated early in the season and didn't slow down even when teams began to double team him.

Nnaji, the Pac-12 Freshman of the Year and a first team all-conference selection, averaged 16.3 points and 8.6 rebounds, while shooting 57 percent for a 21-11 team. The Wildcats defeated Washington, 77-70, in the first round of the Pac-12 tournament before it was canceled. I felt Arizona would have made the brackets for the seventh time in eight years.

Arizona State (20-11) earned its third straight 20-win season and was on the verge of its third consecutive NCAA bid for the first time since the early 1960s. One-time Duke All-American point guard Bobby Hurley has enjoyed his time in Tempe. Junior guard Remy Martin, who earned first team

All-Pac 12 honors, averaged 22.6 points with eight 20-point games in the Sun Devils' 11 true road contests.

USC went 22-9, its fourth 20-win season in five years, as Andy Enfield continued to make the Trojans a consistent winner, closing on a three-game win streak. The Trojans had one of the under-the-radar diaper dandies in 6'9" Onyeka Okongwu, who was a two-time California Player of the Year as a freshman and sophomore at Chino Hills, California. He missed his junior year with an injury and was not selected to any of the brand name High School All-American games despite putting up big numbers on the Adidas summer circuit.

It didn't take long for Okongwu to become the Trojans best all-around player. He averaged 16.2 points, 8.6 rebounds, and shot 61.6 percent from the floor, which had to make NBA scouts salivate.

Colorado (21-11) was ranked for much of the season and enjoyed a 69-67 win over Dayton on a neutral site in Chicago, handing the third-ranked Flyers one of their two losses. The Buffaloes started the season 14-3 but limped home 7-8 in its final 15 contests, including a five-game losing streak. Tad Boyle's club had one of the best backcourts in the country with McKinley Wright, who averaged 14.4 points, and Tyler Bey, who averaged 13.8 points.

Stanford (20-12) was right on the bubble but suffered a bad 63-51 loss to California in the opening round of the Pac-12 tournament, taking the Cardinal off the bubble.

The league also had one of the most disappointing teams in America. Washington had two potential NBA first-round picks in 6'9", 240-pound, freshman center Isaiah Stewart, and 6'9" forward Jaden McDaniels. The duo combined to average 30 points, yet the Huskies finished 15-17, including an eight-game losing streak. The team was not the same following the departure of Kentucky transfer Quade Green, a point guard who averaged 11.6 points in 15 games, before being declared academically ineligible.

Overall, it was a great season for the Pac-12. Commissioner Larry Scott had to be thrilled with the results.

# CHAPTER SIXTEEN

---

# WHAT HAPPENED TO NORTH CAROLINA?

The University of North Carolina has always been one of the bluest of the blue bloods in college basketball. But the Tar Heels, who have won three national championships and nine ACC regular season titles since 2005 under Hall of Fame coach Roy Williams, suffered through injuries to key players and an unexpected collapse. The slide included eight losses of four points or less and left them with a 14-19 record, a tie for 13th in the Atlantic Coast Conference regular season, and an 81-53 loss to Syracuse in the second round of an abbreviated ACC tournament.

The meltdown left them on the outside looking in at the NCAA tournament and gave Williams, who had taken North Carolina to 15 NCAA tournaments in 16 years, his first losing season in 32 years at Kansas and North Carolina.

"I didn't enjoy it at all," Williams said. "I really didn't. I lost weight, more than I ever lost during a basketball season. I slept less than I ever have and I don't sleep a lot. It was a hard year. We had a lot of injuries. We didn't play well and I didn't coach as well as I wanted to, but it was not much fun other than trying every day. And I love trying to do the best I can and trying to get the kids to do the best they can. I don't think we ever gave up. It looked like it in some ways in the Syracuse game in the ACC tournament. That's the reason why I wish, if they were going to call it off, they'd call it off 18 hours earlier."

North Carolina lost all five starters, including three who were selected in the first round of the 2019 NBA draft—6'8" fifth-year senior forward Cameron Johnson, freshman point guard Coby White, and freshman small forward Nassir Little—and not everybody can recover that quickly.

North Carolina was ranked ninth in the AP preseason poll filled with nine teams that had won national championships, and Williams signed a franchise player, Cole Anthony, a McDonald's All-American from Oak Hill Academy (Virginia), a diaper dandy and a big time player, at their biggest position of need.

Anthony didn't take long to make an impact in his college debut.

He had an incredible game, set the school record for scoring by a freshman, finishing with 34 points and 11 rebounds, while leading the Tar Heels past Notre Dame, 76-65, in their opener at Chapel Hill. With his father—former UNLV and NBA guard Greg Anthony, in the stands, the ACC preseason Freshman of the Year broke Rashad McCants' 17-year old scoring record in his first game and finished 12-for-24 from the field with six three-pointers.

It looked like they were headed for a quality season. I saw this team play twice in the Battle4Atlantis tournament in the Bahamas. The Tar Heels battled Michigan, but fell short. Then North Carolina got past a very good Oregon team. Fast forward to a game I called between North Carolina and Florida

*Roy Williams suffered through a challenging season at Chapel Hill.*

State, and it was shocking to realize how this season turned out. A lot had to do with the fact the Heels shot 42 percent from the field, their worst season since going 41.3 in 1960 under Frank McGuire. The team made just 30.4 percent of its three-point shots. The offense was limited. UNC averaged 85.8 points in 2019 during its Sweet 16 season and only 72 points this year. That was the fewest points per game since putting up 71.4 in 1999 under Bill Guthridge.

You have wonder whether things might have changed if Anthony had been healthy all season. He was the heart and soul of that team. Nine games into the season, Anthony missed a 68-64 upset loss to Wofford with an injured right knee that sidelined him indefinitely. By the time he returned, Carolina had struggled through a 4-7 stretch that defined their season. Carolina, which has average talent by its standards, was also forced to play games without guard Leaky Black and without Brandon Robinson, who can put points on the board.

There just weren't enough personnel to overcome that loss.

Williams became so frustrated at one point in January, he went on his radio show and called his team the least talented he had coached at UNC. He was just being honest and up front. That was not vintage North Carolina.

"I've had teams with four, five, or maybe six McDonald's All-Americans on the team," he said. "That is one way to judge the talent coming in. I'm not saying it is good or bad, but Cole was hurt at the time so 6'9" freshman forward Armando Bacot was the only McDonald's All-American who we had on the court."

North Carolina did have a chance at some redemption during a long season when the Tar Heels hosted seventh-ranked, neighborhood rival, Duke, at Smith Center. Anthony had 24 points and 11 rebounds for the Tar Heels, who were in control most of the way, then let the game slip away, 98-96, in overtime. Duke rallied from 13 down in the final four-and-a-half minutes of regulation, forcing overtime when sophomore All-American guard Tre Jones hit a jumper at the buzzer.

UNC still looked like it might still win the game in overtime when it took a five-point lead with 20.5 seconds left to play. But Duke found a way to ruin their night when freshman Wendell Moore scored on a game-winning follow-up on a missed shot by Jones at the horn.

"If you don't care who won the game, you had to enjoy that as a big-time college basketball game," Williams said. "I care who won the game, so I did not enjoy the final outcome."

This was a season to forget, historic in negative ways: it was only the second time in 55 years the Tar Heels failed to win 15 games.

North Carolina's fifth losing season in the last 70 years:

| | |
|---|---|
| 1951 | 12-15 |
| 1952 | 12-15 |
| 1962 | 8-9 |
| 2002 | 8-20 |
| 2020 | 14-19 |

North Carolina's malaise shouldn't last long. They are looking like they're going to be back quickly. Looking ahead to 2020-2021, the Tar Heels should have a more talented team, complete with high-end freshmen talent and some veteran presence. Starters Garrison Brooks, Black, and Bacot are all expected to return along with reserves Andrew Platek and Anthony Harris. UNC will add several five-star recruits—6'11" Walker Kessler, 6'10" Day'Ron Sharpe, and guard Caleb Love, along with four-stars R.J. Davis and Puff Johnson in a Top-three class. They're really going to be dynamite. They're going to be playing with a chip on their shoulder and be back where they belong, with all the upper-echelon teams in the ACC.

# CHAPTER SEVENTEEN

# WCC IS MORE THAN JUST GONZAGA

I've traveled to Las Vegas to call the West Coast Conference tournament for many years now.

Little did I know the conference tournament title game between St. Mary's and Gonzaga would be my last game of the 2019-2020 season that I would analyze for ESPN because of the COVID-19 Pandemic.

Bob Wischusen, our play-by-play announcer, my wife Lorraine, and I saw Rod Stewart in concert a few days before the final at Caesar's Palace. Why do I bring that up? He did a song called, "Some Guys Have All the Luck." I thought the WCC fell into that category, stronger and deeper than in recent years.

Second-ranked Gonzaga (31-2) will always be Gonzaga, a perennial national contender that has made it to the conference tournament finals for 23 straight years. And the Bulldogs lived up to that billing, defeating St. Mary's, 84-66, in the championship game to earn a likely No. 1 seed out West. But BYU (24-8) and St. Mary's (26-8) were both Top 30 in the NET and made my Vitale bracket. Six teams in the WCC won 20 or more games.

BYU had a great season under first-year coach Mark Pope, who came over from Utah Valley State when Dave Rose resigned. The Cougars had one of the best seasons in program history—highlighted by a Top 25 ranking for the first time since 2011, a nine-game win streak, and a likely single-digit seed in the NCAA tournament.

Who knows how good the Cougars might have been if 6'8" senior forward Yoeli Childs, their star player for the previous two years, was able to play for the whole season. Childs, who averaged 22.2 points and nine rebounds and shot 57.4 percent and 49 percent from the three, toyed with the idea of

*Saint Mary's Athletics / Tod Fierner*

*Jordan Ford averaged 21.9 ppg. for the Gaels.*

declaring for the draft after the coaching shift. He signed with an agent before filling out the proper documentation, which is an NCAA violation. Childs pulled out of the draft after going through the workout process. The NCAA allowed him to return after a nine-game suspension at the start of the season.

BYU lost eight times and Childs was only on the court for three of those games, all away from home and all by only one point or in overtime. BYU lost to Gonzaga by 23 without Childs and beat the Bulldogs by 13 in Provo with Childs, who went for 28 points and 10 in that game. Childs gave BYU the big man they desperately needed.

The Cougars got the most out of seven seniors during a season when they finished 18th in the AP poll. Point guard TJ Haws averaged 14 points and versatile Jake Toolson, with his 6'5" wingspan, came over from Utah Valley to BYU with Pope, averaged 15.2 points and 4.8 rebounds, and joined Childs on first team All-WCC.

The Cougars never made it to the WCC championship game. Jordan Ford saw to that. Ford, a 6'2", two-year All-WCC guard from St. Mary's, averaged 21.9 points, 4.9 rebounds, and shot 41.9 percent from the three. He had a spectacular tournament for Randy Bennett's Gaels, who won the WCC tournament in 2019.

Ford made two dramatic game-winning shots, as St. Mary's defeated sixth-seed Pepperdine with explosive guard Colbey Ross and third-seed BYU, to return to the title game. He scored 42 points in 50 minutes, including the last seven of the game, making a 30-foot, turnaround three to seal an 89-82, double-overtime win against Pepperdine in the quarterfinals, to offset 43 points by Ross.

Then, after being quiet in the first half against BYU, Ford led St. Mary's back from an 11-point deficit in the second half, hitting a pull up jumper with 1.4 seconds to play for a 51-50 victory to send his team to a third championship game in four years.

Gonzaga also had to work hard to get to the finals, escaping San Francisco (22-12), 81-77, in the semi-finals. Guard Joel Ayayi scored 12 of his 14 points in the second half. The redshirt sophomore from Bordeaux, France broke a 69-69 tie with 4:14 left with a jumper, and hit a mid-range shot on the following possession to give the Bulldogs a 73-69 lead over a team that played them within four points during the regular season. Ayayi scored eight of Gonzaga's nine points during a 9-3 run.

San Francisco had a strong season, and I was so impressed with coach Todd Golden. He was so organized and optimistic about his team. Guard Charles Minlend scored 19 for the Dons but they fell just short.

"I'm proud of the way our guys competed," Golden said. "On a big stage, with a Gonzaga-dominated crowd, withstanding an early rally they had, we competed."

With 22 wins, San Francisco tied the 2017-2018 team for the program's most wins in a season since the Dons brought the once-fabled Bill Russell-fueled program back to life in 1985.

*BYU's Jake Toolson averaged 15.2 ppg. and 4.8 rpg.*

This is going to be a wild league in the future. Gonzaga will still be the team to beat, but more and more teams are edging into contention. Pacific was the surprise team and coach Damon Stoudamire, a former NBA player, won the WCC Coach of the Year after leading the Tigers to its most successful season in recent history in his fourth season. In his first year with full scholarship support, he took a team filled with question marks—picked to finish in a tie for eighth place in the preseason poll—to a 23-9 record and a share of third place with an 11-5 mark, getting the most from his three guards—Gary Chivichyan, Justin Moore, and Jahlil Tripp—and a deep bench. Tripp scored a career-high 39 in a 107-99 four-overtime win against St. Mary's. Chivichyan also came up huge, hitting shots to force a third and fourth OT, then making two game-sealing free throws.

Gonzaga led the nation in scoring points per game:

Gonzaga—87.4
Duke—82.5
Alabama—82.0
Green Bay—81.6
Winthrop—81.3

# CHAPTER EIGHTEEN

# MARYLAND SURGING UNDER TURGEON

When Maryland's Hall of Fame coach Lefty Driesell took the head coaching basketball job at that ACC program in 1970, one of the first things he did was announce his goal was to make the Terrapins "The UCLA of the East."

Driesell signed enough blue-chip prospects like Tom McMillen, Len Elmore, John Lucas, Buck Williams, and Len Bias. The Terrapins were a fixture in the AP Top 10, but he never made an NCAA Final Four.

Maryland has only been to the Promised Land twice, in 2001 and in 2002, when Hall-of-Fame coach Gary Williams won a national championship.

It's been a while since Maryland fans had a true nationally-elite team to root for. I think Mark Turgeon gets a lot of heat from those fans. I think they would have been a threat in the tournament and they had some tremendous wins. I don't know what they could have been upset about? I'll tell you what I think it is: people get spoiled. Maryland fans had an incredible love affair with Gary Williams. And then you have a new guy and, unless he's going to do wonders or cut down the nets, it's never going to be good enough.

*Maryland Athletics*

*Turgeon has recorded winning seasons in all nine years at Maryland.*

This team had that potential to meet expectations. Maryland was picked seventh in the AP preseason poll and climbed as high as three during the regular season. The Terrapins opened the season 10-0 with wins over Marquette, Notre Dame, and Illinois. They enjoyed an eight-game winning streak in the league from January 18 to February 18 and finished 24-7, winning a share of the Big Ten championship at 14-6, along with Michigan State and Wisconsin. But they had to scramble down the stretch to make it happen after blowing a two-game lead with five to go after losing three of four games. They had to defeat Michigan, 83-70, in the last game of the season to finish 16-1 at home and earn their first title since moving to the Big Ten in 2014.

*Cowan averaged 16.7 points, 34.7 minutes, 4.7 assists, and 81.1 percent from the line.*

"We had it hanging over us for two weeks," Turgeon said. " We were in first place for almost four weeks. There was a lot on our guys and obviously this was a big weight off us."

The Terrapins had one of the dynamic duos in college hoops in senior guard Anthony Cowan Jr. and 6'9" sophomore forward Jalen "Sticks" Smith.

*The dynamic duo of Cowan and Smith.*

The 6'0" Cowan, who returned to Maryland for his final year to hang a banner, was a workhorse from St. John's of Washington, D.C., starting every game of his 130-game career. He is the only player in Maryland history to lead the program in scoring, assists, minutes, steals, and free throw percentage for three straight seasons. Cowan was a clutch shooter who averaged 16.7 points, 34.7 minutes, 4.7 assists, 1.0 steals, and 81.1 percent from the line as a senior, when he was selected first team All-Big Ten.

Smith, a third team AP All-American from Mt. St. Joseph's in Baltimore—who averaged 15.5 points—was the first Terrapin named to the AP first, second, or third team since Greivis Vásquez earned AP second team honors in 2010. He was first team All-Big Ten and a first team All-Big Ten Defensive team selection.

On the season, Smith tallied 21 double doubles (third nationally), including 13 in his final 14 games, the fourth-most in Maryland single season history. Smith ranked second in the Big Ten in rebounds (10.5) and blocked shots (2.4), in addition to ranking fourth in field goal percentage (.538).

Maryland also got double-figure scoring from 6'6" sophomore Aaron Wiggins, who averaged 10.4 points, and was part of a talented, deep perimeter that featured Cowan. The lineup also included three-point shooter Eric Ayala (8.5 points) and defensive standout Darryl Morsell. They could match up with any team in the country. The only thing missing was an accomplished post player to replace 6'10" NBA draft pick Bruno Fernando's low post scoring.

*Jalen Smith was a double-double guy (15.5 ppg., 10.5 rpg.).*

As successful as the Terrapins were, they also had their moments of inconsistency. Maryland scored 70 or more points in their first nine games. They were held to below 70 in 11 of their final 22.

This was a team that played hard every night, something Turgeon could be proud of. They had numerous comeback victories and the confidence was there. They knew they could get to the winner's circle.

One great example occurred February 26 during a 74-73 victory over Minnesota. Down 17 late in the first half, the Terrapins used a never-say-die attitude and fought back. Morsell drained the go ahead three-point jumper with 1.9 seconds left to complete the comeback.

Maryland last made the Sweet 16 in 2016, losing to Kansas, 79-63. There was a belief the Terrapins could make the Final Four and cut the nets down again in Atlanta, the same city where they won it all.

This season, those dreams died hard.

# CHAPTER NINETEEN

# LEGENDARY COACHES DANCE AGAIN

I was really excited about this big dance because I thought about the amazing coaching talent in my field.

No book on a virtual NCAA tournament would be complete without mention of Duke's Hall-of-Fame coach Mike Krzyzewski. Coach K, who played for Bob Knight at Army, is a member of my Mt. Rushmore of great college coaches. He has won five national championships in 1991, 1992, 2001, 2010, and 2015—second only to the late John Wooden of UCLA—in his 40 years at Duke and has led the Blue Devils to 12 Final Fours, 15 ACC championships, and 12 ACC regular season titles.

Krzyzewski has also coached the U.S. men's national basketball team to three gold medals in the 2008, 2012, and 2016 Summer Olympic Games. He was also an assistant coach on the 1992 Dream Team. Krzyzewski has won a record 1,281 career games. He is a two-time inductee into the Naismith Hall of Fame—in 2001 for his individual coaching career and in 2010 as part of the collective induction of the Dream Team.

Duke has only been to the Final Four twice in the past 10 years, but the Blue Devils are a perennial national contender. Duke finished 23-7

Reagan Lunn/Duke Athletics

*Coach K was looking forward to his 36th NCAA Tournament appearance.*

and was ranked 11th in the AP poll with a young team that had to replace three 2019 NBA first-round draft picks but still managed to finish in a tie for second in the ACC. They depended heavily on 6'10" center Vernon Carey Jr. and point guard Tre Jones, both All-Americans, and freshman guard Cassius Stanley, who could join them as a first-round pick.

When glancing at the projected 2020 field, there were so many teams and coaches ready to provide excitement. This had to be a potentially special big dance, Awesome With a Capital A!

The great programs are always judged by how they do in the NCAA Tournament. The Blue Devils were expected to be a factor in March Madness again.

At the start of the 2020 season, there were eight schools that had won at least three championships.

11 UCLA, 1964-1995.

8  Kentucky, 1948-2012.

6  North Carolina, 1957-2017.

5  Duke, 1991-2015.

5  Indiana, 1940-1987.

4  Connecticut, 1999-2014.

3  Kansas, 1952-2008.

3  Villanova, 1985-2018.

Six of those eight teams were expected to be in this year's 68-team field.

*Wright is 28-14 lifetime in the NCAA Tournament.*

(Connecticut and North Carolina fell short in my bracket.)

The 2020 big dance was expected to be filled with coaches who have lots of experience in the tournament. Five have made at least 20 trips.

35 Mike Krzyzewski with Duke, 1984-2019.

24 Bob Huggins with Akron, Cincinnati, and West Virginia, 1986-2018.

22 Tom Izzo with Michigan State, 1998-2019.

21 Bill Self with Tulsa, Illinois, and Kansas, 1999-2019.

20 Mark Few with Gonzaga, 2000-2019.

Coaches with most Final Four appearances (five or more).

12 Mike Krzyzewski, Duke (1986, 1988, 1989, 1990, 1991, 1992, 1994, 1999, 2001, 2004, 2010, 2015).

12 John Wooden, UCLA (1962, 1964, 1965, 1967, 1968, 1969, 1970, 1971, 1972, 1973, 1974, 1975).

11 Dean Smith, North Carolina (1967, 1968, 1969, 1972, 1977, 1981, 1982, 1991, 1993, 1995, 1997).

9  Roy Williams, Kansas, North Carolina (1991, 1993, 2002, 2003 with Kansas; 2005, 2008, 2009, 2015, 2017 with North Carolina).

8  Tom Izzo, Michigan State (1999, 2000, 2001, 2005, 2009, 2010, 2015, 2019).

6  Denny Crum, Louisville (1972, 1975, 1980, 1982, 1983, 1986).

6  Adolph Rupp, Kentucky (1942, 1948, 1949, 1951, 1958, 1966).

5  Jim Boeheim, Syracuse (1987, 1996, 2003, 2013, 2016).

5  Bob Knight, Indiana (1973, 1976, 1981, 1987, 1992).

5  Guy Lewis, Houston (1967, 1968, 1982, 1983, 1984).

5  Lute Olson, Iowa, Arizona (1980 with Iowa; 1988, 1994, 1997, 2001 with Arizona.

5  Rick Pitino, Providence, Kentucky, Louisville, (1987 with Providence; 1993, 1996, 1997 with Kentucky; 2005, 2012*, 2013* with Louisville).

   *Vacated

*Izzo was looking for his ninth Final Four appearance.*

MSU Athletics Communications

Four coaches with at least 20 straight tourney trips.

24 Mike Krzyzewski, Duke (1996-2019).

22 Tom Izzo, Michigan State (1998-2019).

21 Bill Self, Tulsa, Illinois, and Kansas (1999-2019).

20 Mark Few, Gonzaga (2000-2019).

Active coaching leaders in tournament winning percentage (minimum 10 games).

.764 (97-30) Mike Krzyzewski, Duke (1984-2019).

.752 (79-26) Roy Williams, Kansas, North Carolina (1990-2019).

.750 (9-3) Chris Beard, Arkansas-Little Rock, Texas Tech (2016-2019)

.734 (47-17) John Calipari, Massachusetts, Memphis, Kentucky (1993-2019).

.712 (52-21) Tom Izzo, Michigan State (1998-2019).

.706 (48-20) Bill Self, Tulsa, Illinois, Kansas (1999-2019).

.667 (16-8) Tony Bennett, Washington State, Virginia (2007-2019).

.667 (10-5) Frank Martin, Kansas State and South Carolina (2008-2017).

.667 (28-14) Jay Wright, Hofstra, Villanova (2000-2019).

Only Williams and Martin missed the Vitale bracket.

Think about it: Coach K, Izzo, Self, Few, Calipari, Wright, Huggins, Bennett, and Hamilton. Seeing these maestros on the sidelines, great basketball minds who teach strategies as well as Xs and Os. They get the most from their talent and consistently win on and off the court. So many great potential coaching matchups were wiped away. Maybe we can enjoy these showdowns in the 2020-2021 big dance, baby!

*Kansas Athletics*

*Self led Kansas to a 28-2 record in its final 30 games.*

# CHAPTER TWENTY

# OH, BROTHER

## The Joneses and the Millers

If the 2019-2020 NCAA tournament had taken place, there were a couple of brother acts—James Jones of Yale and Joe of Boston University, as well as Sean Miller of Arizona and Archie of Indiana—that would have made for some great storylines!

Let's start in New Haven, Connecticut, where James Jones was ready to lead Yale back into the tournament. Jones, who was born in Long Island, played college basketball at SUNY Albany and worked as a sales executive for NCR before beginning his coaching career. He succeeded Dick Kuchen as head coach of Yale in 1999. He is the all-time winningest men's basketball coach at Yale, winning Ivy League championships in 2016, 2019, and 2020, upsetting Baylor in the first round of the 2016 NCAA Tournament.

In the last four years, the Bulldogs won 79 games and posted a remarkable 39-17 Ivy League record. 6'10" junior center Paul Atkinson had a special season for Yale. Atkinson was the co-Ivy League Player of the Year with Penn forward AJ Brodeur. He led the league in field goal percentage (.630), was third in scoring with 17.9 points per game, fifth in rebounding with a 7.3 rebounding average, seventh in steals with 1.2 per game, and 10th in blocked shots with 0.8 per game. Atkinson had 20 or more points 12 times and scored double figures in every game of Yale's 23-7 season, which included wins over Clemson and Vermont and a three-point loss to North Carolina. In 14 Ivy games, he averaged 18.6 points and 7.5 rebounds.

*Yale Athletics*

*James Jones was ready for his third career NCAA Tournament appearance.*

Yale was awarded the NCAA berth because it won the Ivy League regular-season title with an 11-3 record. The conference canceled its four-team tournament, which may have been a big break for the Bulldogs. The tournament was going to be hosted by Harvard, which had beaten Yale twice in the regular season, including a 14-point win in the regular season finale.

Joe was a year younger and the two played one year in the same backcourt in high school. Joe played for Oswego State and stayed in school an additional two years to get his masters' degree in counseling before getting into college coaching as an assistant at Hofstra and Villanova. He then became head coach at Columbia, which was in the same league as Yale. They spent seven years competing against each other before Joe, who was getting worn out from the experience, took a job as an assistant to Steve Donahue at Boston College in 2010. He then moved after a year to become the head coach at Boston U.

This was Joe's most surprising and most successful season. The third-seeded Terriers were the surprise winners of the Patriot League, defeating Colgate, 64-61, before a sellout crowd of 1,724 at tiny Cotterell Court in Hamilton, New York, in the tournament championship game. Junior forward Max Mahoney, who won the tournament MVP award, scored 18 points, and had the 20th double-double of his career, keyed the upset and gave BU its first automatic NCAA berth in nine years.

The Terriers (21-13), who started the season 3-7 with a win over South Carolina, went 18-6 in their last 24 games, defeating the defending, top-seeded Raiders, which had beaten them twice during the regular season and were 15-1 at home, by limiting them to just 4-of-22 three pointers.

The other brother act includes Sean Miller and younger brother Archie. They grew up in a basketball family. Their father, John, was an iconic high school coach at Blackhawk near Pittsburgh; he went 657-230 in a 35-year coaching career. He won eight Western Pennsylvania Interscholastic Athletic League championships, four Pennsylvania Interscholastic Athletic Association titles, and he taught his sons how to coach. Sean was a celebrity at a young age, a ball-handling prodigy who appeared on *The Tonight Show Starring Johnny Carson* when he was 14 years old, and his skills were such that he was featured in the 1979 movie, *The Fish That Saved Pittsburgh*, starring Julius Erving. Sean was a four-year starting point guard at Pittsburgh before getting into coaching.

The 51-year old elder Miller coached Xavier to three Atlantic 10 regular season titles and four NCAA appearances from 2005 through 2009. Then he moved to Arizona, where he brought that once-fabled program back to relevance, winning 30 games and advancing to the 2012 NCAA Elite Eight in his second year. Miller, a three-time Pac-10 Coach of the Year, had taken the Cats to seven NCAA appearances, three Elite Eights, and two Sweet 16s.

Sean is no stranger to controversy. He is currently the subject of a reported investigation related to the 2017 NCAA basketball corruption scandal regarding offers to illegally pay athletes for attending his school, including 2017 recruit and future No. 1 NBA draft pick DeAndre Ayton. He has denied any allegations against him.

Sean Miller coached Arizona to a 21-11 record this season. The Wildcats were ranked for much of the season and were 10-8 in an improved Pac-12. Guards Nico Mannion—who has dual citizenship in the U.S. and Italy—and Josh Green from Australia, along with forward Zeke Nnaji, gave Miller a trio of superb diaper dandies. All three have declared for the NBA draft and could be first round picks.

Archie Miller is 10 years younger than Sean. After Sean graduated Pittsburgh, he took a job as an assistant at North Carolina State and recruited Archie to be Herb Sendek's point guard.  He has been an older brother and a mentor as Archie climbed the coaching ladder. Archie Miller took Dayton to four NCAA appearances and an Elite Eight in six years in his first head coaching job, then took the Indiana job in 2017.

Indiana University Athletics

After 16-15 and 19-16 seasons, the 41-year-old Miller looked like he was on the verge of a breakthrough year. The Hoosiers finished with a 19-12 record, and Miller had the Hoosiers in position for their first NCAA berth since 2016, when they made the Sweet 16.

Diaper Dandy Trayce Jackson-Davis, the 6'9" son of former NBA star Dale Davis, led the Hoosiers, averaging 13.5 points. Indiana closed 5-8 in its last 13 games and finished 9-11 in league play, leading some, including ESPN bracketologist Joe Lunardi, to question whether Indiana would go dancing. *I had them in.*

*Archie Miller was preparing for Indiana's first NCAA Tournament appearance since 2016.*

So did Miller, who went on a rant after a late season loss to Wisconsin. He defended his team's resumé with a strange "Sesame Street" analogy that included a swipe at bracketology, and Lunardi in particular.

"It's a children's show," Miller said. "Every bracketology is a children's show. Bottom line with our resumé (is) it's strength of record, and that's undeniable." The Hoosiers had quality wins over Florida State, Iowa, Penn State, Ohio State, and Michigan State.  "If you beat six or seven guys in the field, you should be in the field," he said.

Then, he took direct aim at Joey Brackets. "You know, when I was in the Atlantic 10, Joe Lunardi was my best friend," Miller said. "He used to help me all the time. When I went to Indiana—he needed to crap on Indiana the other day just so people would watch 'Sesame Street,' you know what I'm saying?"

Miller clearly wasn't happy with what he described as "Sesame Street cartoon guys on TV who need people to click," bad-mouthing his team's credentials.

As of the Monday before the Big Ten tournament, Indiana was No. 29 in the country in strength of record and No. 13 in strength of schedule, per ESPN. Lunardi had Indiana among his "Last Four in."

Oh, brother, two great storylines to follow in the tournament.

| ARCHIE | | SEAN |
|---|---|---|
| 9 | SEASONS | 16 |
| 194-106 | W-L | 404-105 |
| 5-4 | NCAA TOURNEYS | 19-11 |
| 6 | 20-WIN SEASONS | 13 |

# CHAPTER TWENTY-ONE

# DAWN STALEY MISSES A CHANCE AT HISTORY

Dawn Staley is the logical choice to become the next great coach in women's basketball, following in the footsteps of Pat Summitt and Geno Auriemma.

The beloved former Philadelphia Dobbins High, Virginia, Olympic, and WNBA star, who was inducted into the Naismith Hall of Fame in 2013, coached the U.S. national team to the 2019 World Championships in the Canary Islands. She also coached South Carolina, which won the NCAA tournament in 2017, to the top of the 2020 AP and USA Today Top 25 polls. She had a chance to pull a rare double in the same calendar year, winning both a national championship and an Olympic World Championship in Tokyo at the 2020 Summer Games...before the devastating COVID-19 Pandemic canceled both events.

*South Carolina Athletics*

*Staley's team closed the season with 26 straight wins.*

Staley's team of six returning players and the nation's top recruiting class entered the season ranked in the Top 10. The Gamecocks spent 10 weeks at the top of the AP poll with the steady leadership of 5'10" guard Tyasha Harris and 6'2" forward Mikiah Herbert Harrigan. The two seniors led the otherwise youthful team to a 32-1 squad record that included 26 consecutive wins to close the regular season, a perfect 16-0 for the program's fifth SEC regular-season championship, and five SEC tournament titles in six years.

Staley challenged her team with the fifth-toughest schedule in the country and the Gamecocks answered with a 13-1 record against nationally-ranked opponents, including wins over three teams that finished the season in the Top 5. South Carolina went 8-0 against RPI Top-25 teams and 8-1 against the next 25 to lock up a No. 1 seed in the NCAA Tournament. They put an exclamation point on their season by beating Connecticut for the first time ever, 70-52, in Columbia, limiting the 11-time national champions to just two points in the first quarter. Harris scored 19 points and 6'5" freshman center Aliyah Boston dominated underneath with 13 points and 12 rebounds.

The SEC and national coach of the Year led a team that embodied her competitive personality and built its success on a commitment to defense and a team-first mentality. The Gamecock offense scored a school-record 82 points per game while no individual Gamecock averaged more than 13.1 points.

*South Carolina Athletics*

*South Carolina was 13-1 vs. nationally-ranked teams under Staley this season.*

South Carolina bench added 26.6 points. Defensively, South Carolina limited opposing teams to just 33.3 percent shooting and grabbed 30.1 defensive rebounds per game.

Staley swept the Coach of the Year awards and was the first person to win the Naismith award as both a player and a coach. She built a national profile as a ball-handling wizard at Dobbins in the Philadelphia Public League and was selected as national Player of the Year. She signed with Virginia, where she played point guard for Debbie Ryan, led the Cavaliers to four Final Fours, and was named national Player of the Year in 1991 and 1992.

Staley became a three-time Olympic gold medalist who was elected to carry the American flag in the opening ceremony at the 2004 Olympics. After winning a gold medal in the 1996 Olympics at Atlanta, she went on to play professionally in the American Basketball League and the WNBA and, in 2011, was voted one of the top 15 players in league history. In 2000, she was attending the Final Four in Philadelphia when she was approached by Temple AD Dave O'Brien about coaching the Owls. At first, she resisted because she was still playing in the WNBA and didn't think she could handle both. But she was intrigued by the challenge and transformed the team into a regional power that went to six NCAA tournaments and four Atlantic 10 titles in eight years.

She rebuilt the South Carolina program from scratch, going from two losing seasons to a No. 1 ranking and a Final Four during the 2015 season. Two years later, the Gamecocks were 33-4, winning the SEC regular season and the conference tournament for a third straight year before advancing to a second Final Four and winning their first national title in school history. 6'5" center A'ja Wilson scored 23 points, grabbed 10 rebounds, and blocked four shots during a 67-55 win over conference rival Mississippi State, 67-55, in the NCAA finals at Dallas.

*Staley led South Carolina to a 32-1 record.*

South Carolina Athletics

That same year, she was named as the U.S. national team coach, a year after serving as Auriemma's assistant on the 2016 Olympic gold medal-winning women's basketball team in Rio. She coached the American team with international Hall-of-Fame stars like Diana Taurasi, Breanna Stewart, and Sue Bird to a 2019 FIBA World Championship, defeating Australia, 73-56, in the gold-medal game. 6'9" Brittany Griner held the Aussies' 6'5" star Liz Cambridge to just seven points.

Staley still has a soft spot for Philadelphia, where she has a mural that was painted in her honor. She gave her 1996 Olympic gold medal to her mother Estelle, whom she cites as the biggest influence in her life.

Dawn currently heads the Dawn Staley Foundation, which gives middle-school children a positive influence in their lives by sponsoring an after-school program at the Hank Gathers Recreation Center in North Philadelphia.

# CHAPTER TWENTY-TWO

# SABRINA IONESCU SETS RECORDS...
# BUT NO TITLE

The biggest news in women's college basketball last year occurred when Oregon's junior point guard Sabrina Ionescu, who would have been the No. 1 pick overall in the 2019 WNBA draft, opted to return to school for her senior year. She wanted to complete "some unfinished business" as she wrote in the *Players' Tribune* after her Ducks lost to eventual champion Baylor in the NCAA Final Four.

Ionescu had the type of epic season that put her in the same category as all-time greats Cheryl Miller of USC, Maya Moore, Diana Taurasi, and Breanna Stewart of Connecticut. She won the Wooden award for a second straight year, as well as every major Player of the Year award. Oregon fans in the Pacific Northwest have started to refer to her as "The G.O.A.T."

The three-time Pac-12 Player of the Year matched her own NCAA single-season record with eight triple-doubles to extend her all-time record *for both men and women* to 26. She became the first player in NCAA history to reach 2,000 career points (2,562), 1,000 assists (1,091), and 1,000 rebounds. Ionescu led the nation with a career-high 9.1 assists per game while averaging 17.5 points and a career-high 8.6 rebounds per game, and was fourth nationally with a 3.05 assist to turnover ratio.

The 5'10" Ionescu starred on a second-ranked 31-2 team that led the country in scoring, averaging 86 points per game

*Ionescu won her second straight Wade Trophy (Player of the Year).*

GoDucks.com

*Ionescu set an NCAA record with 26 double-doubles.*

with a scoring margin of 28.1 points and was a likely No. 1 seed in the NCAA tournament's West Region. Ionescu shot 51.8 percent and a Pac-12-leading 92.1 percent from the line.

Ionescu grew up the daughter of Romanian immigrants in Walnut Creek, California, across the bay from San Francisco. She attended Miramonte High School, where she was a four-year varsity player. Ionescu played for USA Basketball, where she won a gold medal in 2014 as a member of the U-17 FIBA World Championship team and emerged as a Top 5 recruit nationally, earning MVP at the McDonald's All-American game after scoring 25 points and grabbing 10 rebounds.

She signed with Oregon over Texas and Washington, even though the Ducks did not have a national profile at the time. She was a star from the start, winning the USBWA national Freshman of the Year Award, and then leading the Ducks to their first ever No. 1 seed in the NCAA tournament. She won her first Wooden award as a junior.

Oregon, top-ranked South Carolina, and defending national champion Baylor were considered the favorites in this year's tournament. Ionescu won the Nancy Lieberman Award as the country's best point guard. Ruthy Hebard won the Katrina McClain award as the best power forward and Satou Sabally won the Cheryl Miller Award as the country's best small forward. Oregon is the first team to have three of the Naismith's starting five winners.

"I've heard some folks say that we're a one-person show," Oregon coach Kelly Graves said. "This just goes to show that, no, we weren't. And I also think it shows this was going to really be a tough team to beat."

Ionescu and Sabally went 1-2 in the WNBA draft.

Ionescu gained some celebrity status this year because of her close personal relationship with the late Kobe Bryant and his 13-year old daughter Gianna. Bryant brought Gigi, and the rest of the Mamba youth travel team he sponsored, up to watch Ionescu play in January of 2019 and came away impressed by her mentality. The two kept in touch and Bryant became a mentor. Last summer, Ionescu traveled to L.A. to coach a few of Gigi's summer league games.

When Bryant, Gigi, and seven others died in a tragic helicopter crash going to a practice near L.A., Bryant's widow asked Ionescu if she would speak at his Memorial Service at the sold-out Staples Center. Ionescu gave a touching eulogy for both, saying she still texts Kobe.

"The texts go through but no response," she said. "It still feels like he's there on the other end. That the next time I pick up the phone, he would hit me back. It's so strange to describe him or Gigi in the past tense. No one teaches you that about grief. If I represented the present of the women's game, Gigi was the future and Kobe knew it."

After an emotionally-draining morning, Ionescu flew to the Bay area for a game against nationally-ranked Pac-12 rival Stanford. After throwing up before the game, she took the floor and threw down a triple double—21 points, 12 rebounds, and 12 assists—during a 74-66 victory.

"That was for him," she told ESPN afterwards. "I know he's up there looking down and he's proud of me."

Bryant was not the only NBA great to notice Ionescu's extraordinary talent. Steph Curry brought his daughters Riley and Ryan to one of Ionescu's games and asked her to pose for a picture with the family. LeBron James, the King, referred to Ionescu as "Queen Sabrina" in one of his admiring tweets.

Ionescu would have been the centerpiece of the women's tournament if it had been played.

*Ionescu was a three-time Pac-12 Player of the Year.*

# CHAPTER TWENTY-THREE

# LONG TIME NO SEE

## Rutgers 1991, Penn State 2011, Illinois 2013

There were a number of teams that were ready to return to the big dance this March after a long absence. Three of them—Rutgers, Penn State, and Illinois—came from the same conference, the Big Ten.

Rutgers was ready to dance for the first time since 1991 when Bob Wenzel coached the Scarlet Knights to a 19-10 record and the Atlantic 10 regular season championship. They lost to Arizona State in the first round of the tournament.

Since then, they have been wandering in a basketball desert without water. They went through five coaches until they found Steve Pikiell, who played for Jim Calhoun at Connecticut and was coaching Stony Brook. Pikiell arrived for the 2016-2017 season. After three straight losing seasons, this year's team enjoyed its first 20-win season since going 20-13 in 2003-2004. They returned to the Top 25 for the first time since 1978-1979. It was Rutgers' first winning season since the Knights were 19-14 in 2005-2006.

The starved fans were going bananas all season, filling up the 8,000-seat RAC ever since the start of Big Ten season. Junior point guard Geo Baker and 6'6" sophomore wing Ron Harper Jr. led this return to prominence. The Knights, who were picked to finish 12th in the league in the preseason poll, didn't have a big scorer, but they had nine guys who could score in a Big Ten game and Pikiell had them defending and rebounding on every possession.

*Geo Baker led Rutgers with 98 assists.*

121

Rutgers Athletics

*Pikiell was ready to take Rutgers to its first NCAA Tournament since 1991.*

The Knights were 17-1 at home. Wins came against Seton Hall, Wisconsin, Penn State, Illinois, Indiana, and Minnesota, but they locked up an at-large bid in my bracket with back-to-back wins over ninth-ranked Maryland and a 71-68 overtime win in a road game against Purdue when Baker made a shot to send the game into overtime, and then made a game-clincher in overtime. The Knights had an NCAA resumé with an 11-9 record in the Big Ten, five quadrant I wins, nine wins against quadrant I and II opponents, a Top-30 ranking in the NET, and four double-digit wins over ranked opponents.

Rutgers fans have been hungry for a competitive national program since 1976 when Phil Sellers, Mike Dabney, James Bailey, Eddie Jordan, and Abdul Anderson led them to a perfect 32-0 regular season and their only trip to the NCAA Final Four.

I'd like to think I played a little role in that.

I got my first start on the collegiate level in 1971 when Howard Garfinkle ("Super Garf") sold me big time to Dick Lloyd, who was the new head coach at Rutgers. Immediately, after accepting the assistant coaching job, I started to recruit in a very aggressive manner, as I wanted to prove that Rutgers could compete for the blue chip superstars in the metropolitan area. The problem at Rutgers when I arrived was they were in a state of shock when I said I wanted to go after the best of the best. The one thing I possessed was my many contacts in the New Jersey area, after having coached at East Rutherford High School, New Jersey; and being fortunate to have won two consecutive state championships. Obviously, a key reason for our success was the sensational play of 6'10" Leslie Cason.

The first two guys that I really wanted were Phil Sellers from Thomas Jefferson High School in Brooklyn, New York, and Michael Dabney, the best player in the state of New Jersey, who starred at East Orange High School, New Jersey. It was a great learning experience working under coach Lloyd, as he was so organized in every facet of the game.

After Lloyd resigned at the end of the 1973 season to go into administration, I was so proud that he strongly recommended me for the head coaching job. I felt so confident that, if given the opportunity, I would not let down the fans of Rutgers University. I pleaded for the job and even offered to do it for the $11,000 I was making as an assistant. But unfortunately for me, the athletic director, Fred Gruninger, had other plans. He hired Tom Young from American University, who certainly was a solid choice.

Then out of the blue, I was offered the head coaching job at the University of Detroit, and I never looked back. It turned out that going to the Motor City was the best thing I ever did, as I met many new people who played a vital role in my career. Our Titan program really began to captivate the people in Motown, and our highlight was making it to the Sweet 16 in 1977, where we lost a

*Ron Harper Jr. led the Scarlet Knights in scoring (12.1 ppg.).*

heartbreaker to the #1 team in the nation, Michigan. Our battle with the Wolverines took place at the Rupp Arena in Lexington, Kentucky. It was the last college game I ever coached.

Young won at Rutgers, but eventually became frustrated after the school turned down a chance to play in the Big East because they thought they would be part of an Eastern all-sports league with Penn State. Young left for Old Dominion. The Knights had a couple moments under Wenzel, but they faded into the background after he left for Jacksonville.

Pikiell has been a breath of fresh air.

Penn State, who once made a Final Four back in 1954 and a Sweet 16 run in 2001, made its first trip to the tournament since 2011 under Ed DeChellis, who promptly departed for Navy after the season. Penn State reached out to Chambers. Chambers is a one-time Jay Wright assistant and head coach of a BU team that won the Patriot League tournament and had just played in the NCAA tournament. It took Pat Chambers nine years to climb this mountain, but the Nittany Lions finally made it to the top, succeeding at a football school. It hasn't been easy. Penn State, finishing last in the league in Chambers' first two years and playing before a half full Jordan Center. Things eventually improved. Chambers coached Penn State to a 26-13 record in 2018, when the Lions won the NIT.

But after guard Tony Carr, the team's top player, bolted early for the pros, Penn State slipped again in 2019, finishing 14-18 after losing their first ten Big Ten games before winning seven of their last 10. Their late-season resurgence convinced 6'8" forward Lamar Stevens to return for his senior year.

"Even through the skid that we hit, I still saw the talent," Stevens said. "We had all the pieces coming back. I felt like I could help that."

Stevens had an all-Big Ten season. He averaged 18 points and 6.8 rebounds, finishing in the Big Ten's Top 10 in both categories. He was the star of an experienced team of three seniors and two junior starters, including 6'9", 250-pound senior center Mike Watkins and junior point defensive Jamari Wheeler, a first team all-conference defensive player. The Nittany Lions finished 21-10 and 11-9 in league play, its first winning record in the toughest conference in the country. Chambers had his team ranked 23 in its first AP Top 25 appearance since 1996 after a win over then fourth-ranked Maryland and a hot 10-2 start.

Penn State rose to #13 after a six-game winning streak in early February that included wins over Michigan State, Michigan, and Indiana. They then lost five of their last six games, including a Senior Night loss to Northwestern. "I'm really proud of what we've done—21 wins, 11 wins in the league," Chambers said. "We played eight teams in the Top 25. I'm not going to diminish or steal the joy from my players or my staff. Am I disappointed (in) how we've finished these games here? Yeah. However, the big picture, macro—these kids have done something Penn State really hasn't seen."

Craig Pessman/Illinois Athletics

*Dosunmu averaged 16.6 ppg.*

Stevens scored over 2,200 points and finished within seven points of becoming the program's all-time scoring leader. "He was the Saquon Barkley for basketball," Chambers said. "He put us on a stage we so desired to be on."

Chambers will include Penn State on the banner in the Jordan Center listing the program's NCAA appearance and find a way to honor Stevens as the program's all-time leading scorer. He would have gotten there with at least one more game.

Illinois would have gone dancing for the first time since 2013. Brad Underwood coached the Illini to a 21-10 record and a fourth-place finish in league play with a 12-6 record, a year after they finished 12-21 and 4-14 in his first year after coming over from Oklahoma State.

The 12 wins was the school's fewest since 1974-1975. Still, there were signs the Illini was on the verge, with wins over 15th-ranked Maryland at the Garden, ninth-ranked Michigan State, and NCAA-bound Ohio State.

The Illini turned things around when versatile 6'5" sophomore guard Ayo Dosunmu became a star who averaged 16.6 points, 4.3 rebounds, and 3.3 assists, shot 48.4 percent and 75.5 percent from the line, and was a first team all-Big Ten selection. 7'0", 290-pound recruit Kofi Cockburn emerged as an impact player who averaged 13.3 points, 8.8 rebounds, and 1.3 blocks, shot 53.2 percent, and was selected as Big Ten freshman of the year. Underwood upgraded his team's defense, which limited opposing teams to just over 65 points per game, and key players found their roles.

"Last year was an inferior season in the sense of the way we produced on the court, but I feel like it was a positive season in the locker room because we had to go through what we went through to get to where we are now and to understand the struggle and the grind and what's at task of winning," Dosunmu said. "We had to go through all that to understand it."

Rutgers, Penn State, and Illinois enjoyed special seasons, even though they did not enjoy an actual dance. Nobody can take away the success and the joy.

# CHAPTER TWENTY-FOUR

# UNSUNG PLAYERS WERE READY

Over the years, the NCAA has produced unsung heroes—players who deserved more ink and stepped up in the big dance.

I think about Stephen Curry, Davidson's magical shooter. He went from being largely ignored by major colleges to becoming the best shooter in college basketball and led the 10th-seeded Southern Conference Wildcats to the NCAA Midwest Elite Eight in 2008. Curry, who led the country in scoring with a 28.6 point average, scored 40 points in the opening round against Gonzaga when he made 8-of-10 three pointers, and then averaged 32 points as the Cats defeated Georgetown and Wisconsin. Davidson came within a missed jumper of beating Kansas in the regional finals.

What about Clinton Ransey and New York City playground legend Mouse McFadden and Cleveland State. Ransey scored 27 points as the 14th-seeded Vikings, a commuter school from Cleveland, and stunned Bob Knight's third-seeded Indiana, 83-79, in a 2006 first-round game. They advanced to the Sweet 16 where they lost to Navy by a single point.

Gordon Hayward was not a big name coming into the tournament, but the 6'9" forward became an important figure in Butler's incredible run to the 2010 NCAA championship game in its hometown. Hayward had a chance to win the game when he launched a half-court shot just before the buzzer of a 61-59 loss to Duke. The shot was online and kicked off the rim. If it had dropped through, it would have replaced Christian Laettner's shot against Kentucky as the greatest in tournament history. Hayward elevated his status with his play and was the ninth pick overall in the NBA draft.

The 2020 tournament would have produced new Cinderella players. Let's look at some of the rising stars from smaller programs.

*Cristian-Jackson averaged 23.5 points and 4.9 assists in league play.*

Akron had a diminutive 5'8", 150-pound guard Loren Cristian Jackson. He was the top player and maestro of a MAC team who averaged 23.5 points and 4.9 assists in league play, while connecting on 59 percent of his 58 attempts from beyond the arc. He had 10 games with 26 or more points.

Jackson is not originally from Ohio. He's been around the country. He was born in Chicago, went to high school at Victory Prep in Florida, and spent his freshman year at Long Beach State, before transferring to Akron, where he has played the last two seasons. He was unstoppable in the second half of a 24-7 season, scoring 35 in a win over Buffalo.

Utah State's Sam Merrill got a lot of publicity out West, but not enough national respect. The 6'5" senior guard, who averaged 19.7 points, made a number of big shots during his career, including drilling a game-winning three-point jump shot with 2.5 seconds left to help his 20-8 team rally from a 16-point deficit to score a stunning 59-56 win over fifth-ranked, 30-2 San Diego State in the Mountain West tournament title game. The league earned a second automatic bid to the tournament.

Merrill, who scored 27 points against the Aztecs, was selected MVP of the tournament for a second straight year. Merrill grew up in Bountiful, Utah, and led Bountiful High to the state championship as a senior. He was recruited by both Stanford and Princeton, but chose Utah State. He went on a two-year Latter-Day Saints mission in Nicaragua before his freshman year and became a four-year starter.

Another player deserving of more ink was redshirt senior Tre Scott, a 6'8" forward who started all 30 games, averaging 11.4 points, 10.5 rebounds, 2.2 assists, 1.5 steals, and 0.8 blocks of Cinncinatti. He was the American Athletic Conference's Defensive Player of the Year, the AAC's Most Improved Player, and the league's Sportsmanship winner on a 20-10 team. He had 13 double-doubles on the season and was the first UC player to average a double-double since Dwight Jones in 1983. Scott played in 108 wins during his career, second behind Steve Logan (111 from 1999-2002). His big game came when he scored 25 points, grabbed 19 rebounds, and hit two threes during an overtime win against Memphis.

Vermont's 6'6" senior Anthony Lamb, one of four finalists for New York's Mr. Basketball. This senior, when he averaged 30 points for Rochester and Greece Athena, has been a dominant force in the

America East for four years. He was born to Rachael Lamb, a union carpenter, when she was just 17 years old, and he grew up without a father. He picked up his work ethic from his mother, who worked 70 hours a week.

As a junior, he was the 2019 America East Player of the Year and an honorable mention All-American when he averaged 21.2 points for a 27-7 NCAA team. Lamb made waves early in his senior year when he scored 23 points, including the game-winning shots over two defenders to take down St. John's. It was the first time Vermont beat a high-major program in over a decade. Lamb then went off for 30 points, including 25 in the second half, during a 61-55 loss to defending national champion Virginia. The Catamounts won the America East regular season and Lamb repeated as Player of the Year after averaging 16.7 points and 7.1 rebounds for a 26-7 team.

These four guys lost out on their shot at being the next Cinderella at the big dance.

*Merrill hit the game-winning shot against San Diego State in the Mountain West final.*

Utah State University Athletics

# CHAPTER TWENTY-FIVE

# EVERYONE LOSES

## How Atlanta Was Clobbered Without the Final Four

I was really looking forward to calling games at the Final Four in Atlanta. I've been broadcasting for ESPN International for several years, usually calling the final week of college basketball with Sean McDonough. This year would have been special because it figured to be one of the wildest Final Fours. So many teams had a legitimate shot to go to Atlanta. All they had to do was get hot at the right time.

This year's Final Four was set to be held at the $1.5 billion Mercedes Benz Stadium in the Centennial Olympic Park section of downtown Atlanta on April 4 and 6, 2020 before it was canceled by the NCAA because of the global coronavirus pandemic. The next six Final Fours will be held at Indianapolis, New Orleans, Houston, Phoenix, San Antonio, and Indianapolis, so the next time Atlanta will be eligible to host a Final Four will be in 2027.

Think about the restaurants and bars that lost major business—the servers, valet parking attendants, cleaning crews, the pain and loss of income they suffered. What about the hotels and their workers who lost so much business revenue? Stores in the area were expecting a big windfall that suddenly disappeared. Airport workers in Hartsfield Airport lost out as well.

I'm heartbroken for everyone who lost so much.

Instead of a celebration, with parties, a coaches' convention, where you saw most Division I coaches in hotel lobbies, and a Fan Fest, where basketball lovers were in paradise, it was all wiped out. I've been to many Fan Fests and loved connecting with fans, young and old.

This is big business. The men's Final Four was expected to produce an economic impact of $100 million this year. The last time it was held in Atlanta, in 2013, it produced an economic impact of $70 million for the city.

Last year, when the men's Final Four was held in Minneapolis, the NCAA earned a reported $933 million in revenue with $800 million coming from broadcast rights and the rest from ticket sales, corporate sponsorships, and TV advertising. The full three-week event accounts for an estimated 75 percent of the governing body's annual revenue, which hit $1.2 billion for the fiscal year, ending on Aug. 31, 2019.

The TV contract between CBS, Turner, and the NCAA, which was extended in 2016 for eight years through 2032, will pay out $1.1 billion per year when the extension kicks in 2024, markedly up from $770 million under the current contract.

A recent story in Forbes mentioned the loss of tourism in the Olympic Park area, which was built for sporting events. It started with the 1996 Olympics, when the park replaced worn-out, dilapidated warehouses and vacant lots. The city started to bet on sports as a tourism driver. Hotels and restaurants started to sprout up around the now torn down Georgia Dome, which was replaced by Mercedes-Benz Stadium.

*Mercedes-Benz Stadium*

*The streets were empty in Atlanta after the big dance was cancelled.*

"We will be severely impacted by the Final Four not going off as planned," said David Marvin, the founder and president of Legacy Ventures, which owns or manages five hotels and 20 restaurants in the Centennial Park area. "We had a lot of cancellations."

Marvin said he was not sure whether business-interruption insurance will apply to the losses around the Final Four.

The number of hotel rooms and fan-friendly venues downtown is frequently mentioned as a reason Atlanta secures so many prime sporting events, like the Final Four, the College Football Playoff, and the Super Bowl. Marvin's company has five of those hotels—American, Embassy Suites, The Hilton Garden Inn, the Glenn, and the Indigo—within walking distance of the arena.

Marvin said if the coronavirus pandemic drags into early summer, it could be similar to the hit taken after 9/11, when all but essential travel was banned. Marvin said that business in March was off 30 percent and 50 percent in April.

Had the tournament gone on as scheduled, the NCAA was anticipating paying out approximately $600 million to Division I schools this year. But, with no tournament, the NCAA announced that figure will be $225 million. The vote by the NCAA Board of Governors was unanimous. The money will be handed out in June—as opposed to the initial timeline of April, and will be done specifically to support college athletes during the uncertainty of the current environment, along with the importance of planning carefully with less revenue.

The NCAA will dip into $50 million of its reserve partners. The organization says it recouped $270 million thanks to its insurance policy. But the lack of revenue stands to be a huge hit with the trickle-down impact on college athletics. In terms of money breakdown, $53.6 million of the $225 million will be split equally among the 32 conferences and teams "that meet athletic and academic standards to play in the men's basketball tournament."

The other near-$172 million will be split up based on factors the NCAA did not reveal. With no men's tournament, the units paid to each league would be severely damaged in both this year and in years to come. The units are paid out on a rolling six-year period, so the cancellation of the tournament leads to lower gains.

Tough times for a lot of people.

This would have been the fifth Final Four hosted by Atlanta. There has been a great history in the first four. It started in 1977 at The Omni. Al McGuire and Marquette cut down the nets, beating Dean Smith and North Carolina, 67-59. Butch Lee (19 points), Bo Ellis and Jim Boylan (14 points each), and Jerome Whitehead (11 rebounds) were outstanding.

A special moment for me and our Titan program was in February—three months before Marquette won the National Championship—we won our 21ast game in a row (a school record), beating one of my idols, coach McGuire, in Milwaukee, with a buzzer shot by our guard, Dennis Boyd.

I was so happy for McGuire. There are so many great memories of coaching against the Hall-of-Famer when I was at Detroit. I also saw McGuire many times during his broadcasting career.

Over the years Al and I had many conversations, and I always got a big laugh out of the fact that he would address me as "Dixie." In fact, when we saw each other when I was working a game for ESPN, he would say to me, "Dixie, you're not a star, a star works less, and makes more!" I would laugh hystericaly.

He was so much fun to be around. I really miss him.

Back to Atlanta's other Final Fours:

The 2002 event was special as Gary Williams and the Terrapins celebrated a 64-52 win over Indiana. 52,647 fans attended the championship game at the Georgia Dome. They saw Juan Dixon score 18 points, hitting 6-of-9 field goals. Lonny Baxter added 15 points and the Maryland defense held the Hoosiers to 10-of-35 on two-point field goals and Indiana made just 2-of-7 free throws.

In 2007, Florida won its second straight championship, beating Ohio State, 84-75. No school has won back-to-back titles since. Al Horford led a balanced attack with 18 points and 12 rebounds as the Gators had four players in double figures.

The Gators were clutch on the foul line, making 22-of-25. It was not easy to get to the winner's circle as Greg Oden scored 25 while Mike Conley added 20. The final drew 51,458 for the title game.

The last Final Four hosted by Atlanta was in 2013. Rick Pitino's Louisville Cardinals beat Michigan, 82-76. That helped Pitino become the only coach to take three different schools to a Final Four. That championship game drew 74,326 fans. Luke Hancock came off the bench to score 22 points, converting 5-of-6 field goal attempts. Peyton Siva added 18 points and the Cardinals hit 8-of-16 three-pointers.

The NCAA later vacated that title.

Now, Atlanta loses another championship event. Hopefully the NCAA committee which decides on future Final Fours will look to take care of Peachtree city soon.

# CHAPTER TWENTY-SIX

# DICKIE V'S 2020 AWARDS

While the NCAA tournament disappeared, I did come up with my All-American teams, Player of the Year, Coach of the Year, and Newcomer of the Year.

Here are my All-American teams:

**First Team**

Obi Toppin, Dayton, 6'9", 220 lbs., Sophomore

Luke Garza, Iowa, 6'11", 260 lbs., Junior

Myles Powell, Seton Hall, 6'2", 195 lbs., Senior

Payton Pritchard, Oregon, 6'2", 195 lbs., Senior

Markus Howard, Marquette, 5'11", 180 lbs., Senior

Devon Dotson, Kansas, 6'2", 185 lbs., Sophomore

**Second Team**

Vernon Carey Jr., Duke, 6'10", 275 lbs., Freshman

Cassius Winston, Michigan State, 6'1", 185 lbs., Senior

Tre Jones, Duke, 6'2", 183 lbs., Sophomore

Udoka Azubuike, Kansas, 7'0", 267 lbs., Senior

Anthony Edwards, Georgia, 6'5", 225 lbs., Freshman

Anthony Cowan Jr., Maryland, 6'0", 170 lbs., Senior

**Third Team**

Daniel Oturo, Minnesota, 6'10", 225 lbs., Sophomore

Nick Richards, Kentucky, 6'11", 244 lbs., Junior

Filip Petrusev, Gonzaga, 6'11", 225 lbs., Sophomore

Jared Butler, Baylor, 6'3", 185 lbs., Sophomore

Lamar Stevens, Penn State, 6'8", 230 lbs., Senior

Jordan Nwora, Louisville, 6'7", 225 lbs., Junior

**Fourth Team**

Precious Achiuwa, Memphis, 6'9", 225 lbs., Freshman

Malachi Flynn, San Diego State, 6'1", 180 lbs., Junior

Jalen Smith, Maryland, 6'10", 215 lbs., Sophomore

Xavier Tillman, Michigan State, 6'8", 245 lbs., Junior

Zavier Simpson, Michigan, 6'0", 190 lbs., Senior

Tres Tinkle, Oregon State, 6'8", 225 lbs., Senior

Now for the awards! This has been an outstanding basketball season. There have been upset cities, close contests, and surprising conference title winners. It has been an exceptionally competitive campaign, even without Selection Sunday and March Madness.

It's time to present my Player of the Year, Newcomer of the Year, and Coach of the Year honors. All categories had several viable candidates and I gave serious thought to the contenders. So, without further ado, the envelope please!

**Player of the Year**

I considered several players, including Luka Garza of Iowa, Obi Toppin of Dayton, Payton Pritchard of Oregon and Myles Powell of Seton Hall. At the end, it really came down to a two-man race between Garza and Toppin.

Both big men had stellar seasons on winning teams. The 6'9" Toppin, a redshirt sophomore, averaged 20 points and 7.5 rebounds for a 29-2 team that won the Atlantic 10, was ranked third in the final AP poll, and was a likely No. 1 seed in the tournament. He scored 20 or more points 16 times, was an absolute dunk monster, and was held to single-figure scoring just once for a team that was likely the conference's first No. 1 seed since St. Joseph's in 2004.

The 6'11" Garza, a junior, played in the toughest conference in America and excelled night in and night out. He averaged just under a double-double with 23.9 points and 9.8 rebounds. He was the only player from a Power 5 conference to average 23 points and nine rebounds for the Hawkeyes, who had a 20-11 record and was 25 in the final AP poll, where six teams from the conference were ranked and three more received votes.

Garza had 11 straight games with 20 or more points against ranked teams, including 44 against Michigan. He was the first Iowa player to score 700-plus points in a single season in school history (his total was 740 points). It was nip and tuck, a true battle of the stars.

And the winner is . . . Luka Garza.

*Luka Garza scored at least 20 points*
*in each of his last 16 games.*

## Coach of the Year

The leading candidates were Scott Drew of Baylor, Brian Dutcher of San Diego State, Anthony Grant of Dayton, and Leonard Hamilton of Florida State.

I cut my list down to two after Baylor, which spent four weeks at No. 1 in the AP poll, dropped three of its last five regular season games. Meanwhile, San Diego State, which once was 26-0, fell twice down the stretch, including the Mountain West title game against Utah State. (Sam Merrill beat the Aztecs with a buzzer three.)

So, it came down to Grant and Hamilton. Dayton set a school record for single-season wins, a tremendous feat considering the fact that Tom Blackburn and Don Donoher both coached there. Florida State finished 26-5 and was ranked fourth in the final AP poll. The Seminoles won the ACC regular season crown for the first time ever with a 16-4 conference record, edging the likes of Louisville, Duke, and Virginia. The Seminoles were picked fifth in the ACC preseason poll! Both Grant and Hamilton had tremendous credentials. It was a tough decision that could have gone either way.

The winner is . . . Leonard Hamilton.

Hamilton had a great season without a true superstar, although 6'9" freshman forward Patrick Williams and 6'6" sophomore guard Devin Vassell, who have declared for the NBA draft, could both be first round picks. No Seminole averaged 13 points per game. But Hamilton's team found ways to win close games. The Seminoles won 11 games by six points or less.

*Hamilton led FSU to 11 wins by six points or less.*

**And, finally, my choice for Newcomer of the Year**

It really came down to two players: 6'10" freshman center Vernon Carey Jr. of Duke and 6'5" freshman guard Anthony Edwards of Georgia. Edwards, who averaged 19.1 points, 5.8 rebounds, 2.8 assists, and 1.3 steals for Tom Crean's SEC team, is a leading candidate to be the top pick in the NBA draft.

Carey meant so much to Duke's 11th-ranked, 25-6 Blue Devils, who finished in a tie for second in the ACC regular season with Louisville and Virginia (despite suffering foul trouble in several contests). He averaged 17.8 points—third in the league—and 8.8 rebounds. He posted 15 double-doubles and shot 57.7 percent to lead the ACC in field goal percentage.

I give the slightest edge to . . . Vernon Carey Jr.

Congratulations to the winners of the Dickie V National Awards—Luka Garza, Leonard Hamilton, and Vernon Carey Jr.!

*Reagan Lunn/Duke Athletics*

*Carey Jr. led the ACC with a .577 field goal percentage.*

# THE 2020 TOURNAMENT

# THE BRACKETS

# THE RESULTS

# ROUND ONE

**EAST**

1 DAYTON
16 BOSTON U/RBT MORS
8 LSU
9 OKLAHOMA
5 MICHIGAN
12 AKRON
4 LOUISVILLE
13 YALE
3 SETON HALL
14 BELMONT
6 BYU
11 INDIANA
7 COLORADO
10 UTAH STATE
2 KENTUCKY
15 ARKANSAS-LITT. RK.

**SOUTH**

1 BAYLOR
16 WINTHROP
8 HOUSTON
9 MARQUETTE
5 WISCONSIN
12 UCLA/NC STATE
4 AUBURN
13 LIBERTY
3 CREIGHTON
14 BRADLEY
6 PENN STATE
11 NORTH TEXAS
7 WEST VIRGINIA
10 ARIZONA STATE
2 FLORIDA STATE
15 NORTH DAKOTA STATE

**WEST**

1 GONZAGA
16 NC CENT/PRAIRIE VW
8 RUTGERS
9 USC
5 OHIO STATE
12 STEPHEN F. AUSTIN
4 OREGON
13 NEW MEXICO STATE
3 DUKE
14 EASTERN WASHINGTON
6 BUTLER
11 EAST TENNESSEE STATE
7 VIRGINIA
10 ST. MARYS
2 SAN DIEGO STATE
15 CAL-IRVINE

**MIDWEST**

1 KANSAS
16 SIENA
8 PROVIDENCE
9 FLORIDA
5 IOWA
12 RICHMOND/TEXAS
4 MARYLAND
13 HOFSTRA
3 VILLANOVA
14 VERMONT
6 ARIZONA
11 CINCINNATI
7 ILLINOIS
10 TEXAS TECH
2-MICHIGAN ST
15-NORTHERN KENTUCKY

# THE RESULTS

The VBDI (Vitale Bald Dome Index) went overtime to produce the results of the 2020 NCAA men's basketball tournament.Here are the results and short game stories from each contest.

# ROUND ONE

## FIRST FOUR

### BOSTON UNIVERSITY 64, ROBERT MORRIS 59

The Terriers won an NCAA Tournament game for the first time since 1959, edging Robert Morris. Rick Pitino, Mike Jarvis, Dennis Wolff, and Patrick Chambers all tried but did not win an NCAA tournament game at Boston University, and the Terriers snapped an NCAA Tournament seven-game losing streak.

Max Mahoney scored 17 points, including four free throws in the final 1:08 for the Terriers. Walter Whyte added 13 for Boston University.

Josh Williams and Dante Treacy led the Colonials with 12 points apiece. Robert Morris (20-15) saw its four-game win streak snapped with the loss.

### UCLA 77, NC STATE 73

Chris Smith and Tyger Campbell scored 14 points apiece to lead four players in double figures as UCLA edged NC State, 77-73.

UCLA earned its first NCAA Tournament win since 2017.

The victory helped Bruins' first-year coach Mick Cronin advance. This marked his 10th consecutive year in the NCAA Tournament.

*UCLA Head Coach Mick Cronin.*

The Bruins rallied from a 31-28 halftime deficit. NC State was led by Devon Daniels with 16 points, while CJ Bryce scored 14.

The Wolfpack's inability to hit three-pointers was a key. NC State made 4-of-21 from beyond the arc, finishing the season with a 20-13 record.

### NC CENTRAL 81, PRAIRIE VIEW 72

The Eagles extended their win streak to seven games with a victory over Prairie View A&M.

Jordan Perkins scored 18 points and CJ Keyser came off the bench to add 17 for North Carolina Central.

The Eagles built up a 13-point lead in the first half and rolled to victory.

The win was North Carolina Central's first NCAA Tournament win since 2014. The Eagles had lost their prior three appearances in the First Four.

Devonte Patterson led the Panthers with 17 points and eight rebounds. The Panthers, which entered the tournament with a 9-2 record in its last 11 games, finished the season 19-14.

### TEXAS 64, RICHMOND 61

In a rollercoaster season, the Longhorns celebrated a big comeback, rallying from a 13-point deficit with 8:37 left to edge the Spiders.

Andrew Jones, who was diagnosed with leukemia in January 2018 but underwent successful treatment, continued his Cinderella season, scoring a game-high 23 points. Matt Coleman added 16 for the Longhorns.

Richmond, which shot 58 percent from the floor in the first half, missed 11 of its last 13 field goal attempts.

Blake Francis led the Spiders with 16 points, while Jacob Gilyard dished out eight assists.

The Spiders finished the season at 24-8.

## EAST FIRST ROUND

### DAYTON 81, BOSTON UNIVERSITY 58

The Flyers continued their magical season with a conniving win over the Terriers. Dayton earned its record 30th win of the season, and 21st in a row.

Obi Toppin posted a double-double with 24 points and 10 rebound*s*, hitting 1-of-11 from the field. Jalen Crutcher and Rodney Chatman added 14 points apiece.

Dayton hit 64 percent from the floor in the first half, building up a 21-point lead at intermission.

Javante McCoy and Jonas Harper led Boston University with 13 points each. The Terriers finished the season at 22-14.

*Dayton's Obi Toppin.*

## LSU 84, OKLAHOMA 80

Javonte Smart scored 24 points and LSU rallied for an 84-80 win over the Sooners.

Oklahoma led 33-32 at half, but failed to hold the lead. Smart had two key baskets in the final 1:15 to help the Tigers.

Kristian Doolittle and Brady Manek led the Sooners with 15 points.

Oklahoma, which started the season 7-1, was .500 the rest of the season (12-12) to finish 19-13. The Sooners are 1-3 in their last four NCAA Tournament games.

LSU won its fifth straight first round NCAA Tournament game.

## MICHIGAN 72, AKRON 61

Juwan Howard won his first NCAA Tournament game as a head coach, leading the Wolverines to a win over the Zips.

Zavier Simpson had 14 points and dished out nine assists. Isaiah Livers and Jon Teske each scored 14 points for Michigan.

The Wolverines secured their fifth straight 20-win season and fourth consecutive NCAA Tournament first round win.

Channel Banks led the Zips with 15 points. Akron saw its three-game win streak snapped and completed the season at 24-8.

## LOUISVILLE 77, YALE 69

Jordan Nwora had 17 points to lead five players in double figures as the Cardinals advanced past the Bulldogs.

One key to the victory was Louisville's dominance on the glass, with a 38-26 rebounding advantage.

Up three with two minutes left, Ryan McMahon hit a key three-pointer to help the Cardinals.

Yale closed the season at 23-8.

## SETON HALL 89, BELMONT 80

Myles Powell scored 31 points as Seton Hall survived a scare in round one.

Belmont hit 14-of-27 from behind the arc to stay close with Seton Hall.

Powell scored 11 of his 31 points in the final 5:35 to get the Pirates to the winner's circle.

Tyler Scanlon Adam Kunkel combined for eight three-pointers for the Bruins, who finished the season at 26-8.

Belmont finished with its 10th straight 20-win season.

The Pirates, ranked as high as eighth in the AP poll this season, moved on to a game against BYU.

## BYU 74, INDIANA 71

The Cougar veterans outshined the youthful Hoosiers in a game that went to the wire.

Yoeli Childs had 23 points and 11 rebounds, Jake Toolson added 18 points and TJ Haws chipped in with 16 points for the winners.

Trayce Jackson-Davis, the son of former NBA star Dale Davis, led the Hoosiers with 22 points.

Indiana last won an NCAA Tournament game in 2016.

*Yoeli Childs of BYU.*

## UTAH STATE 68, COLORADO 63

Sam Merrill continued his hot streak, scoring 24 points as the Aggies upset the Buffaloes.

It was Merrill's fourth straight game with at least 24 points.

Utah State rolled to its 10th win in its last 11 games.

McKinley Wright led Colorado with 16 points. The Buffaloes finished the season 21-12.

## KENTUCKY 74, ARKANSAS-LITTLE ROCK 62

John Calipari moved to 10-0 in first round NCAA Tournament game at Kentucky. Immanuel Quickley, who was held below 20 points in his prior three games, scored 22 in the victory.

The Wildcats reached the 26-win mark for the seventh straight year.

Kentucky held Arkansas-Little Rock to 38 percent from the floor.

# SOUTH FIRST ROUND

## BAYLOR 64, WINTHROP 51

The Bears held an opponent below 55 points for the 10th time this season.

Jared Butler scored 16 points and Freddie Gillespie grabbed nine rebounds and blocked five shots for the Bears. Baylor earned a first round NCAA Tournament win for the second straight season.

Winthrop saw a five-game *win* streak snapped as Hunter Hale scored a team-high 12 points.

The Eagles finished the season at 24-11.

## HOUSTON 69, MARQUETTE 66

Quentin Grimes hit the game-winning three-pointer with 3.2 seconds left to give the Cougars the victory. The winning shot offset a brilliant performance by Markus Howard in his final collegiate game.

Howard scored 35 points, including eight three-pointers.

DeJon Jarreau scored 15 points and Grimes added 14.

The Cougars moved to 11-3 in its last 14 games.

Marquette lost its fourth straight game and completed the season at 18-13.

*Marquette's Markus Howard.*

*Marquette Athletics*

## UCLA 63, WISCONSIN 60

Cody Riley had a season-high 22 points as UCLA stunned Big Ten regular season co-champion Wisconsin.

Brad Davison led the Badgers with 15 points, while Micah Porter added 12.

UCLA held Wisconsin to just 34 field goal percentage in the second half.

Wisconsin saw an eight-game win streak snapped and finished the season 21-11.

## AUBURN 81, LIBERTY 77

In the 2019 NCAA men's basketball tournament, Auburn won its first round game vs. New Mexico State by one point, 78-77.

Bruce Pearl's Tigers survived another scare, edging Liberty by four. Samir Doughty hit four free throws in the final 48 seconds and finished with 21 points.

Scottie James led the Flames with 18 points.

Liberty finished with a school-record 30 wins (30-5). The Flames saw a three-game win streak snapped in its second straight NCAA Tournament trip.

*Auburn's Samir Doughty.*

## CREIGHTON 70, BRADLEY 64

In a battle of a former Missouri Valley Conference member against a current one, the Bluejays advanced.

Ty-Shon Alexander led a balanced attack with 16 points. Creighton was without injured starter Marcus Zegarowski, sidelined with a knee injury.

The Braves were looking for their first NCAA Tournament win since 2006. Elijah Childs led Bradley with 16 points.

Bradley enjoyed its third straight 20-win season and finished 23-12.

## PENN ST 67, NORTH TEXAS 63

Penn State of the Big Ten was challenged by Conference USA champion North Texas.

The Mean Green led 32-31 at halftime.

Lamar Stevens scored 14 of his team-high 16 points in the second half.

Deng Geu led a balanced North Texas lineup with 14 points.

The Mean Green started the season 2-5 and came on, finishing the season 20-12.

## WEST VIRGINIA 69, ARIZONA STATE 67

The Mountaineers, after a 21-loss season last year, earned a hard-fought first round win over Arizona State.

Emmitt Matthews hit two free throws with 8.3 seconds left to lock up the win. Remy Martin hit a three-pointer at the buzzer to make the final margin two points.

Matthews and Derek Culver led Mountaineers with 15 points.

The Sun Devils struggled on three-pointers, hitting just 4-of-22.

Arizona State made the NCAA Tournament for the third straight year.

## FLORIDA STATE 66, NORTH DAKOTA STATE 55

The ACC regular-season champion moved to 7-1 in its last eight games. Devin Vassell scored 14 points and Trent Forrest added 13.

Florida State held North Dakota State to 38 percent from the field.

Tyson Ward led the Bison with 16 points. North Dakota State saw a five-game win streak snapped, finishing the campaign at 25-9.

*Devin Vassell of Florida State.*

## MIDWEST FIRST ROUND

### KANSAS 74, SIENA 55

The Jayhawks continued a pair of big streaks in a win over the Saints.

Kansas won its 14th straight first-round NCAA Tournament game; its last first-round loss came in 2006 vs. Bradley, 77-73.

The Jayhawks extended their current win streak to 17 games. Udoka Azubuike remained an unstoppable force inside, hitting 9-of-10 shots, finishing with 22 points and nine rebounds. Devon Dotson contributed 19 points.

Jalen Pickett scored 14 points to lead Siena. The Saints were held to 36 percent shooting from the floor.

Siena, which saw a 10-game win streak snapped, finished the season at 20-11.

### FLORIDA 77, PROVIDENCE 74

Andrew Nembhard hit the game-winning three-pointer with 3.5 seconds left. Nembhard and Noah Locke led the Gators with 16 points each, while Kerry Blackshear scored 15 while grabbing nine rebounds.

Alpha Diallo led the Friars with 24 points.

Florida won a first-round tournament game for the fourth straight season.

The Friars had a six-game win streak snapped and finished the season at 19-13.

### IOWA 68, TEXAS 61

Luka Garza continued to state his case for National Player of the Year, scoring 27 points while grabbing 13 rebounds in a win over Texas.

The performance marked the 17th straight game that Garza scored at least 20 points.

Iowa built up a 12-point first half lead, but

*Devon Dotson of Kansas.*

*Luka Garza, Maishe Daily, and Coach McCaffery of Iowa.*

the Longhorns battled back behind the surprising play of Courtney Ramey, who entered with 10 points in his last three games. Ramey scored 19 against the Hawkeyes.

Iowa, which entered the contest with a two-game losing streak, won its NCAA Tournament opener for the fourth straight time. The Hawkeye last lost an NCAA Tournament first round game in 2014.

## MARYLAND 74, HOFSTRA 67

The tandem of Anthony Cowan and Jalen Smith led the Terrapins to victory over the stubborn Pride.

Cowan led Maryland with 23 points, while Smith added 16 points and nine rebounds.

The win gave Mark Turgeon 25 victories for the fourth time as Terrapins coach.

Desure Buie led the Pride with 19 points, while Eli Pemberton added 16.

Maryland won the game on the foul line, hitting 19-of-22 free throws, while Hofstra made 8-of-11.

The Terrapins won an NCAA first-round game for the second straight season. Hofstra saw its four-game win streak snapped and completed the season at 26-9.

*Anthony Cowan of Maryland.*

Maryland Athletics

## VILLANOVA 81, VERMONT 67

Collin Gillespie led five players in double figures with 17 points as the Wildcats won an NCAA first-round game for the eighth straight season.

Vermont lost its third straight first-round NCAA Tournament contest.

Anthony Lamb completed his college career with a game-high 21 points for the Catamounts.

The Wildcats relied on the three-pointer in the victory, hitting 11-of-26 from beyond the arc.

## CINCINNATI 64, ARIZONA 62

John Brannen's first NCAA Tournament game as Cincinnati's head coach was a success.

The Bearcats rallied from an 11-point first half deficit to upset Arizona, 64-62.

While Jarron Cumberland struggled (six points, 3-of-11 from the field), Tre Scott stepped up to lead Cincinnati with 17 points.

Nico Mannion led Arizona with 19 points.

Cincinnati's defense in defying the three-point shot was key as the Wildcats shot 4-of-23.

### TEXAS TECH 67, ILLINOIS 63

The Red Raiders, after making a run to the national championship game last year, started this season's tournament with a hard-fought win over tenacious Illinois.

Davide Moretti, who struggled with free throws late in losses to DePaul and Kentucky, made all four of his free throw attempts in the final 1:14.

The Red Raiders snapped a regular season-ending four-game losing streak.

Ayo Dosunmu led the Illini (21-11) with 22 points.

### MICHIGAN STATE 70, NORTHERN KENTUCKY 55

Cassius Winston would not allow his college career to end.

He scored a game-high 22 points while dishing nine assists as Tom Izzo, in his 23rd straight NCAA Tournament, earned his 53rd tourney victory.

Xavier Tillman chipped in with 16 points and eight rebounds.

Northern Kentucky was paced by Tyler Sharpe with 14 points. The Norse finished the campaign at 23-10.

## WEST FIRST ROUND

### GONZAGA 80, NORTH CAROLINA CENTRAL 63

Mark Few's 21st consecutive appearance in the NCAA Tournament started successfully as Filip Petrusev scored 23 points and grabbed 11 rebounds.

The WCC champions have now won 12 straight NCAA Tournament first-round games. The Zags last lost an NCAA Tournament opener in 2008.

Gonzaga scored at least 80 points for the 26th time this season.

## RUTGERS 70, USC 69

The Scarlet Knights, in their first NCAA appearance since 1991, won when Jacob Young tipped in a Geo Baker miss with 1.3 seconds left.

Rutgers, which won 20 games for the first time since 1982-83, held USC to 37 field goal percentage.

Jonah Matthews led the Trojans with 18 points.

USC saw its three-game win streak snapped and finished the season at 22-10.

## OHIO STATE 54, STEPHEN F. AUSTIN 50

The Buckeyes scored the game's final seven points to escape with a win over the pesky Lumberjacks.

Neither team shot 40 percent from the floor in an intense defensive battle.

Duane Washington Jr. led the Buckeyes with 14 points while Kaleb Wesson added 13.

Kevon Harris scored a game-high 17 points for the Lumberjacks.

Stephen F. Austin saw a 15-game win streak snapped and suffered just its fourth loss of the season (28-4).

*Geo Baker of Rutgers.*

## OREGON 74, NEW MEXICO STATE 62

Payton Pritchard continued his college career, falling just short of a triple-double with 19 points, eight rebounds, and 11 assists.

The loss snapped the Aggies' 19-game win streak.

Trevelin Queen led New Mexico State with 19 points. The Aggies completed the season at 25-7.

The victory extended Oregon's current win streak to five games.

## DUKE 80, EASTERN WASHINGTON 69

The combination of Vernon Carey Jr. and Tre Jones led Duke to a convincing win.

Carey Jr. scored 18 points and grabbed 11 rebounds, despite foul trouble in the first half; Jones added 16 points and nine assists.

The victory added to Mike Krzyzewski's recon, with 98 NCAA Tournament wins.

The Blue Devils won their 13th straight NCAA Tournament first-round game. Duke last lost an NCAA opener in 2007, falling to VCU.

## EAST TENNESSEE STATE 62, BUTLER 61

Isaiah Tisdale hit a 15-foot jump shot with 6.3 seconds left to give the Bucs the upset victory.

Lamar Baldwin's game-winning shot attempt hit the rim and fell off at the buzzer.

Steve Forbes' team won its 13th straight game and 31st of the season. East Tennessee State won its first NCAA Tournament game since 1992, when it stunned Arizona. The Bucs had lost their last five NCAA Tournament games.

Butler hit 6-of-25 three-pointers in the loss.

## VIRGINIA 55, ST. MARY'S 49

The Cavaliers began defense of the national championship with a tight win over the Gaels.

Kihei Clark scored 15 points and Mamadi Diakite added 14 for the winners. Virginia won its ninth straight game and held an opponent below 50 points for the 13th time this season.

Jordan Ford led St. Mary's with 16 points.

## SAN DIEGO STATE 62, CAL-IRVINE 59

Malachi Flynn hit three free throws in the final 1:16 to give the Aztecs the win.

*Virginia's Kihei Clark.*

With the score tied at 54, KJ Feagin hit a three-pointer to give San Diego State a lead it would not relinquish.

The Aztecs earned their first NCAA Tournament win since 2015.

Evan Leonard led the Anteaters with 14 points.

Cal-Irvine finished the season at 21-12.

*Malachi Flynn of SDSU.*

# THE RESULTS

## ROUND TWO

### EAST SECOND ROUND

DAYTON 77, LSU 72

The Flyers earned a school-record 31st win of the season as Obi Toppin had 19 points and seven rebounds.

Dayton advanced to the Sweet 16 for the first time since 2015. Ibi Watson added 14 points.

LSU was led by Trendon Watford with 17 points, while Skylar Mays added 15.

Dayton led 32-31 at half and went on a 14-5 run over a five-minute span to break the game open.

The Tigers completed their season with a 22-11 record.

*Dayton celebrates.*

LOUISVILLE 70, MICHIGAN 65

In a rematch of the 2013 national championship game, history repeated itself.

Ryan McMahon hit four free throws in the final 52 seconds to secure the Cardinal win. Jordan Nwora led Louisville with 18 points.

Jon Teske had 16 points and Eli Brooks added 15.

The Cardinals advanced to the round of 16 for the first time since 2015. Michigan ended Juwan Howard's first year as head coach at 20-13.

## SETON HALL 91, BYU 87

In a wild, wide-open offensive game, the Pirates outscored the Cougars team.

Myles Powell scored 35 points, including seven three-pointers, while Quincy McKnight added 19.

Jake Toolson led the Cougars with 27 points, while TJ Haws scored 19.

Both teams shot over 50 percent from the floor.

Seton Hall had its second-highest scoring game of the season, putting up 105 vs. Wagner in the season opener.

BYU, in its first season under coach Mark Pope, finished the season 25-9.

## KENTUCKY 71, UTAH STATE 59

John Calipari's defense found a way to slow down Sam Merrill in check.

The Aggies star was held to 14 points on 4-of-13 field goal shooting.

Immanuel Quickley and Tyrese Maxey combined for 35 points (Quickley 18, Maxey 17).

Nick Richards blocked five shots.

The Wildcats advanced to the Sweet 16 for the fourth straight year.

Utah State finished the season 27-9. The Aggies made the second round of the NCAA Tournament for the first time since 2011.

## SOUTH SECOND ROUND

## BAYLOR 70, HOUSTON 63

In a battle of former SWC foes, the Bears escaped with a tight win.

The Bears defense showed added intensity, holding the Cougars to 27 points in the second half.

The game was surprisingly high-scoring in the first half, tied 36-36 at intermission.

Mark Vital led a balanced attack with 14 points. Four Bears scored in double figures.

Quentin Grimes led the Cougars with 20 points.

## AUBURN 74, UCLA 62

Bruce Pearl's team relied on the three-pointer, hitting 14-of-29 to get past UCLA.

The Bruins were in their third game of the tournament and fatigue appeared to be a factor.

J'Von McCormick and Danjel Purifoy each scored 15 points to lead the Tigers.

Auburn made the Final Four last season. The Tigers clinched back-to-back Sweet Sixteen appearances for the first time since 1985 and 1986.

*Auburn Head Coach Bruce Pearl.*

## CREIGHTON 73, PENN STATE 65

The Bluejays advanced to the Sweet 16 for the first time since 2014 with a victory over the Nittany Lions.

Ty-Shon Alexander paced Creighton with 17 points. Christian Bishop, who had 11 points in his prior three games, tallied 12.

Lamar Stevens became Penn State's all-time leading scorer, finishing his career with 22 points. He entered the game just seven points short of the record.

Mike Watkins added 13 points for the Nittany Lions.

Penn State, which earned its first NCAA win since 2011, completed its season at 22-11.

## FLORIDA STATE 72, WEST VIRGINIA 63

In a battle of veteran coaches with over 500 wins, Leonard Hamilton's Seminoles beat Bob Huggins' Mountaineers.

Devin Vassell, M.J. Walker, and Patrick Williams scored 13 points each to lead a balanced attack.

Oscar Tshiebwe led the Mountaineers with 14 points while Jermaine Haley added 13.

West Virginia finished the season with a 22-11 record.

## MIDWEST SECOND ROUND

### KANSAS 67, FLORIDA 49

The Jayhawks used a tenacious defense in the second half to break open a close game. The Jayhawks forced nine turnovers, leading to 14 points after intermission.

Kansas led 31-27 at halftime.

Devon Dotson scored 23 points while Udoka Azubuike grabbed 13 rebounds.

Florida struggled shooting the three-pointer, making 3-of-19.

Keyontae Johnson was the only Gator in double figures with 12 points.

Florida finished the season at 20-13.

The Jayhawks advanced to the Sweet 16 for the ninth time in 10 years.

### MARYLAND 73, IOWA 71

After the teams split two regular season meetings decided by double figures (Iowa 67-49, Maryland 82-72), the Terps won the rubber match.

Aaron Wiggins hit a 15-foot jumper with 2.7 seconds left to give the Terps the victory.

Anthony Cowan led Maryland with 22 points. Luka Garza continued his streak of 20-plus point games to 18, tallying 23.

### VILLANOVA 77, CINCINNATI 64

In a battle of one-time Big East schools, Jay Wright's team advanced to the Sweet 16 for the fifth time in the last seven years.

The Wildcats relied on the three-point shot, hitting 13-of-22. Saddiq Bey had 21 points while Jeremiah Robinson-Earl added 14 points and 12 rebounds.

*Anthony Cowan and Maryland Head Coach Mark Turgeon.*

Maryland Athletics

Jarron Cumberland, who struggled in the first-round game, bounced back and led the Bearcats with 22 points. Keith Williams added 12 points.

AAC regular season co-champion Cincinnati completed John Brannen's first season as head coach at 21-11.

MICHIGAN STATE 81, TEXAS TECH 69

In a rematch of last year's national semifinal, Michigan State avenged its Final Four loss.

This time around, the Spartan offense clicked, shooting 54 percent from the field (32-of-59 field goals). In last year's Final Four, the Spartans shot 32 percent from the field and totaled 51 points.

Cassius Winston led Michigan State with 18 points. Rocket Watts added 16, and Aaron Henry chipped in with 14 points and seven rebounds.

Jahmi'us Ramsey and Terrence Shannon Jr. led the Red Raiders with 16 points.

Coach Tom Izzo locked up his 14th trip to the Sweet 16.

## WEST SECOND ROUND

GONZAGA 77, RUTGERS 69

Rutgers' dream season came to a halt as Filip Petrusev was too much for Gonzaga.

Petrusev, the WCC Player of the Year, scored 24 points on 10-of-12 shooting from the field. Killian Tillie added 18 points while Ryan Woolridge dished out seven assists with zero turnovers.

The Scarlet Knights, in their first NCAA Tournament since 1991, were led by Ron Harper Jr. with 18 points.

Gonzaga dominated on the glass, with a 37-22 rebound edge.

The Zags made the Sweet 16 for the 10th straight season.

OREGON 67, OHIO STATE 63

The Ducks advanced to the Sweet 16 for the second straight year with a win over the Buckeyes.

Dana Altman moved to 7-0 in NCAA Tournament second round games at Oregon. The Ducks won their sixth straight contest behind Payton Pritchard's 18 points and seven assists.

Chris Duarte added 15 points and seven rebounds, while UNLV transfer Shakur Juiston scored 13 points.

Kaleb Wesson had 17 points and nine rebounds to lead the Buckeyes.

## DUKE 68, EAST TENNESSEE STATE 64

The Blue Devils had a battle against the Cinderella Bucs.

Tre Jones broke a 58-58 tie with a 15-foot jump shot with 1:22 left. Wendell Moore and Cassius Stanley each hit two free throws in the final minute to clinch the victory.

Duke took advantage of a free throw advantage which helped. The Blue Devils made 17-of-19 from the foul line while East Tennessee State was 8-for-12.

Bo Hodges led the Bucs with 14 points while Trey Boyd added 13.

East Tennessee State finished an impressive season at 31-5.

## VIRGINIA 61, SAN DIEGO STATE 57

The Cavaliers relied on defense once again, upsetting the second-seeded Aztecs.

Kihei Clark hit a key basket with 1:35 left and added four free throws in the final minute.

San Diego State was held to 38 field goal percentage (23-of-60) from the field.

Malachi Flynn led San Diego State with 19 points.

Virginia, the defending national champion, advanced to the Sweet 16.

*Matt Riley/Virginia Athletics*

*Kihei Clark.*

# SWEET SIXTEEN

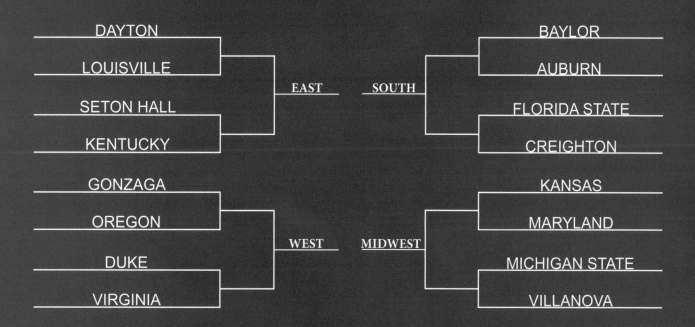

DAYTON

LOUISVILLE

EAST

SETON HALL

KENTUCKY

BAYLOR

AUBURN

SOUTH

FLORIDA STATE

CREIGHTON

GONZAGA

OREGON

WEST

DUKE

VIRGINIA

KANSAS

MARYLAND

MIDWEST

MICHIGAN STATE

VILLANOVA

# THE RESULTS

## SWEET SIXTEEN

### EAST SWEET 16

DAYTON 72, LOUISVILLE 66

The Flyers advanced to the Elite Eight for the first time since 2014, earning a school-record 32nd win of the season.

Obi Toppin had 17 points and 11 rebounds, Jalen Crutcher tallied 16 points, and Trey Landers added 13 for the winners.

Steven Enoch led the Cardinals with 16 points. Jordan Nwora, who picked up two fouls in the first four minutes, scored 11 of his 13 points in the second half. Ryan McMahon added 11 points.

Louisville was held to 38 field goal percentage.

The Cardinals finished the season at 26-8.

*Jalen Crutcher of Dayton.*

Erik Schelkun, Elsestar Images

SETON HALL 67, KENTUCKY 60

Myles Powell duplicated a December 2018 performance vs. Kentucky. He led the Pirates to an 84-83 overtime win that night, with 28 points.

This time Powell had 24 points, including five three-pointers. Myles Cale chipped in with 16 points.

Nick Richards led the Wildcats with 26 points, scoring often inside and drawing Seton Hall's big men into foul trouble.

Seton Hall made the Elite Eight for the first time since 1991, under PJ Carlesimo.

## SOUTH SWEET 16

BAYLOR 68, AUBURN 62

After making the Final Four last season, the Tigers fell just short this time around.

Jared Butler led a balanced Bears attack with 15 points. MaCio Teague added 13 points and Devonte Bandoo added 12.

Samir Doughty led the Tigers with 16 points while Austin Wiley dominated the glass with 13 rebounds.

Auburn was hampered by inconsistent three-point shooting, hitting 6-of-22.

Baylor advanced to its first Elite Eight since 2012.

FLORIDA STATE 67, CREIGHTON 56

Devin Vassell was the only Seminole to score in double figures, putting up 24 points. Florida State's balance was evident as four other players each scored seven points.

The key to the win was three-point shooting as the Seminoles hit 10-of-22 (45 percent). The team made 15 two-point field goals and seven free throws.

Creighton was held to 6-of-26 on three-pointers.

Ty-Shon Alexander led the Bluejays with 16 points.

The Bluejays, the Big East regular season co-champion, finished at 26-8.

## MIDWEST SWEET 16

KANSAS 74, MARYLAND 71

Marcus Garrett hit the game-winning three-pointer with 4.4 seconds left to give the Jayhawks the win.

Anthony Cowan's attempt to tie from three-point range hit off the front of the rim at the buzzer.

The game was nip-and-tuck though, with each team's biggest lead being six points.

Devon Dotson led Kansas with 17 points while Udoka Azubuike added 14.

Cowan led Maryland with 19 points, while Darryl Morsell added 13.

## MICHIGAN STATE 67, VILLANOVA 63

In a battle of teams that finished the season ranked in the AP Top 10, Michigan State and Villanova battled to the wire.

Cassius Winston's college career was extended another game thanks to his brilliant late performance.

Winston made two key passes which led to layups by Xavier Tillman and Gabe Brown as the Spartans hung on.

Collin Gillespie led the Wildcats with 18 points while Jeremiah Robinson-Earl added 14.

"Winston would not let us lose," Tom Izzo said.

The game pitted national championship coaches in Izzo and Jay Wright and it lived up to its billing.

The Wildcats finished the season 26-8.

# WEST SWEET 16

## GONZAGA 77, OREGON 72

In a rematch from an early-season showdown in the Bahamas (Gonzaga won 73-72 in overtime), the Zags moved on in similar fashion.

In the first meeting, Filip Petrusev had 22 points while Corey Kispert added 17. This time, Kispert was the high scorer with 23 while Petrusev added 17.

Payton Pritchard led the Ducks with 18 points, while Chris Duarte chipped in with 16.

Neither team shot 40 percent from the floor in the first meeting (Gonzaga 39, Oregon 34).

The Zags improved to 45 percent (22-of-49) to earn the win.

The Ducks finished the season at 26-8.

## DUKE 64, VIRGINIA 53

This was a rematch of an ACC regular season showdown, won by Virginia, 52-50. In the contest, Vernon Carey Jr. had 17 points and 10 rebounds, while Tre Jones added 17.

Those were the only Duke players in double figures. Cassius Stanley shot 1-of-9 from the field.

Three Cavaliers scored in double figures in that win—Jay Huff (15), Mamadi Diakite (14), and Braxton Key (14).

This game was different. Carey Jr. led the Blue Devils with 19 points, Jones added 15, but it was Stanley who made a difference with 11 points and 4-of-6 field goal shooting.

This time the Cavaliers had two in double figures—Key with 17 and Diakite with 15.

One aspect which was the same, Jones' defense on Kihei Clark. In the first meeting, he shot 2-of-9 from the floor. In the Elite Eight, he was 1-of-6.

Turnovers were another key. Virginia lost 16, Duke turned it over just 11 times.

The loss guaranteed there will be a new national champion. Florida 2006-2007 remains the last team to defend the national championship.

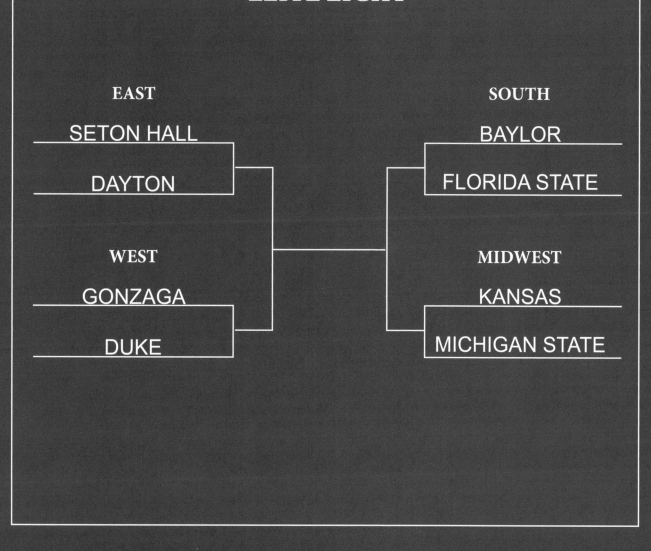

# ELITE EIGHT

**EAST**

SETON HALL

DAYTON

**WEST**

GONZAGA

DUKE

**SOUTH**

BAYLOR

FLORIDA STATE

**MIDWEST**

KANSAS

MICHIGAN STATE

# THE RESULTS

## ELITE EIGHT

### EAST ELITE EIGHT

SETON HALL 73, DAYTON 70

The East regional battle featured two of the premier players in America in Dayton's Obi Toppin and Seton Hall's Myles Powell.

*Courtesy of Seton Hall Athletics*

*Myles Powell.*

Both enjoyed excellent performances during the NCAA Tournament, and they did not disappoint here.

Powell scored 35 points, including seven three-pointers. Toppin posted an impressive double-double with 24 points and 14 rebounds.

"Myles was the man tonight and I am so thrilled his dream of the Final Four came true," Seton Hall coach said.

Turnovers were a factor in Seton Hall's win. The Pirates turned the ball over nine times, seven fewer than Dayton.

While Powell was the star, Quincy McKnight was vital in crunch time with nine points in the last 12 minutes.

"This was a fantastic season, and I'm sorry for the kids that we were short of the Final Four," Dayton coach Anthony Grant said. "I'm so proud of their effort through the entire season."

Dayton, trying to make its first Final four since 1967 (when they lost to UCLA in the title game), finished the season at 32-3.

The Flyers lost their third straight regional final, also losing in the Elite Eight in 1984 and 2014.

Seton Hall, in its first Elite Eight game since 1991, earned its first Final Four berth since 1989. That year the team lost to Michigan in Seattle.

## SOUTH ELITE EIGHT

FLORIDA STATE 68, BAYLOR 61

Scott Drew and Leonard Hamilton were finalists for the National Coach of the Year.

This time out, Hamilton won the prize, a Final Four trip.

Florida State advanced to its first Final Four since 1972 (when they lost to UCLA in the championship game). This is the Seminoles' second Final Four appearance.

*Leonard Hamilton.*

Hamilton has led the Seminoles to the Elite Eight twice in the last three years. This time, he was successful, and depth played a factor.

With the score tied at 57, M. J. Walker hit a three-pointer to give the Seminoles a lead they would not relinquish.

"We have so many players capable of stepping up and making a big shot and today it was M. J.," coach Leonard Hamilton said.

Florida State got a big effort from Malik Osborne with 12 points and 10 rebounds.

Jared Butler and Davion Mitchell led the Bears with 14 points each.

"Give credit to Florida State," Baylor coach Scott Drew said. "They made the big plays down the stretch and we could not get it done. I am so proud of this group and believe we can do more big things next season."

The Bears fell short of their first Final Four since 1950. This was their third Elite Eight loss since 2010 (2010, 2012).

Baylor finished the season at 29-5.

## MIDWEST ELITE EIGHT

MICHIGAN STATE 70, KANSAS 66

In a battle of Hall of Fame coaches, Tom Izzo advanced to his ninth Final Four, getting past Bill Self's Jayhawks.

IZZO IN FINAL FOUR:

1999 Lost to Duke, national semifinals

2000 Beat Florida for national championship

2001 Lost to Arizona, national semifinals

2005 Lost to North Carolina, national semifinals

2009 Lost to North Carolina, national final

2010 Lost to Butler, national semifinals

2015 Lost to Duke, national semifinals

2019 Lost to Texas Tech, national semifinals

2020 ???

*Michigan State coach Tom Izzo.*

MSU Athletics Communications

Foster Loyer hit a three-pointer to break a 51-51 tie and Rocket Watts, Malik Hall, and Kyle Ahrens each hit two free throws in the final 1:07 for the Spartans.

Cassius Winston led Michigan State with 17 points. Xavier Tillman contributed 11 rebounds.

Kansas, which finished the season as the top-ranked team in the AP poll, was led by Devon Dotson with 16 points, Udoka Azubuike, added 15 and Christian Braun added 12.

"This was a classic Sweet 16 game," Izzo said. "Both of these teams played their hearts out. I really respect Coach Self and his team."

"We had our chances, but Michigan State made their free throws late," Self stated. "This was a special team and a special season. I'm sorry we missed out on the Final Four, but a salute to Michigan State."

Michigan State shot 44 percent from the floor while Kansas converted 42 percent. Both teams hit six three-pointers. Free Throws were one difference as the Spartans made 15-of-17 while Kansas hit 11-of-16.

This marks the second straight year Michigan State is in the Final Four.

The Jayhawks fell just short of their second Final Four in three years, finishing the season at 31-4.

## WEST ELITE EIGHT

GONZAGA 74, DUKE 69

It was a rematch of the 2018 Maui Invitational final, with a similar result with even more at stake.

In a showdown at Hawaii, Duke entered as the nation's top-ranked team. The Blue Devils lost as an 89-87 loser.

Duke had a 20-11 free throw advantage to stay in that game. Stars like Zion Williamson, RJ Barrett, Cam Reddish, Rui Hachimura, and Brandon Clarke went on to the NBA.

Tre Jones scored 17 points and Filip Petrusev scored 11 in that contest.

This time around, Petrusev score 21 points while Corey Kispert added 13. Tre Jones and Vernon Carey Jr. led Duke with 16.

The Blue Devils used an advantage on the foul line to stay in the game. Duke was 24-of-31 from the foul line, while Gonzaga made 14-of-18.

The Zags made 51.3 percent from the field to advance.

"It was a treat to go up against a legend in Mike Krzyzewski," Mark Few said. "I was thrilled with the composure we showed."

"Petrusev was very good inside today," added Krzyzewski. "I thought he was the Most Outstanding Player out there.

"Our kids played hard. We had a young team on the court, but I am so proud of them."

*Mark Few, Head Coach of Gonzaga.*

Gonzaga, which enjoyed its fourth straight 30-plus win season, advanced to its second Final Four in four years. The Zags lost to North Carolina in the 2017 national championship game.

Duke lost in its third consecutive Elite Eight. The Blue Devils fell short of their first Final Four since 2015. Krzyzewski's team concluded their season with a 28-7 record.

# FINAL FOUR

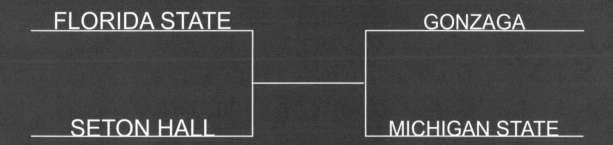

FLORIDA STATE

SETON HALL

GONZAGA

MICHIGAN STATE

# THE RESULTS

## FINAL FOUR

### NATIONAL SEMIFINALS

FLORIDA STATE 72, SETON HALL 71

For the third time in four years, a national semifinal game was decided by one point.

In 2017, North Carolina beat Oregon, 77-76.

Last year, Virginia edged Auburn, 63-62 on Kyle Guy's three free throws in the final seconds.

RaiQuan Gray converted a missed shot by Devin Vassell, getting a layup with 3.3 seconds left to give Florida State a berth in Monday's final.

Myles Powell's desperation 35-foot shot hit the rim at the end of regulation.

Vassell and M.J. Walker led the Seminoles with 14 points each. Powell scored 22 points, 14 in the second half, to lead the Pirates.

Seton Hall's frontcourt was hampered when Sandro Mamukelashvili picked up two fouls in the first 4:38.

"Gray did a great job boxing out on that last play," Leonard Hamilton said during the post-game press conference.

*Coach Hamilton.*

The Seminoles led 36-31 at halftime, holding Seton Hall to 37 field goal percentage.

After containing Powell for much of the first half, the senior hit his first four shots in the second half to give Seton Hall a 46-42 lead.

*Devin Vassell.*

Vassell rallied Florida State with nine points in the second half.

"I was happy for Vassell," Hamilton said. "He has worked so hard all season long."

"Our kids played their hearts out and Powell was a star the way he was all season long," Seton Hall coach Kevin Willard said.

Florida State reached the national championship game for the first time since 1972. The Seminoles lost to UCLA in the championship game that season.

Seton Hall reached its first Final Four since 1989. The Pirates finished the season at 25-10.

## MICHIGAN STATE 81, GONZAGA 79

The Spartans advanced to their third national championship game under Tom Izzo, edging Gonzaga as Rocket Watts hit a driving layup with six second left to break a 79-all tie.

Corey Kispert's 14-foot jump shot at the buzzer would have tied the game, but it hit the rim and bounced away.

"I thought he (Kispert) had it," Gonzaga coach Mark Few said.

"Watts was not the first option to be honest," Izzo stated. The play was designed for Cassius Winston with Watts and Aaron Henry as second options. Gonzaga did a great job on Winston, and we did a great job being flexible to adjust."

Winston led Michigan State's balanced attack with 16 points. Henry had 14, while Xavier Tillman had 13 points and nine rebounds.

Drew Timme and Admon Gilder had their best games of the NCAA Tournament; Timme scored 17, Gilder 16. Filip Petrusev chipped in with 13 points but was held to 4-of-13 field goal shooting.

The Spartans did a great job doubling up on Petrusev, denying him open shots.

"Our gameplay was to slow Petrusev down," Izzo added. "We felt he was vital to their offense. Gonzaga is a very solid offensive team with six guys scoring in double figures. It was not easy to concentrate on one or two people. I thought we held Kispert in check too."

The two national semifinals marked the first time since 2004 that both games were decided by two or fewer points. That year, Georgia Tech beat Oklahoma State, 67-65, and Connecticut edged Duke, 79-78.

Gonzaga fell short of its second championship game in four years. The Zags finished the season at 35-3.

*Phil Ellsworth / ESPN Images*

*Michigan State Head Coach Tom Izzo.*

# THE RESULTS

## THE NATIONAL CHAMPIONSHIP

### FLORIDA STATE 74, MICHIGAN STATE 70

The ACC vs. the Big Ten.

The ACC prevailed.

Florida State won its first national title, beating Michigan State in a thriller in Atlanta on Monday night.

Trent Forrest led a balanced Florida State attack with 15 points, including four free throws in the final 36 seconds to secure the title.

Devin Vassell added 14 points and was named Final Four Most Outstanding Player.

Cassius Winston, in his final college game, led the Spartans with 17 points and 7 assists.

Incredibly, the 2020 Final Four marked the first time in NCAA history that the two national semifinals and the championship game were all decided by four points or fewer. The selection committee had to be thrilled hearing that statistic.

"There is no better feeling than cutting down the nets and hearing 'One Shining Moment,'" Forrest said. "This team has worked so hard this season. We found a way to win in so many close games."

*Ross Obley*

*Trent Forrest.*

*FSU Head Coach Leonard Hamilton.*

"This team was so deep and so many different guys stepped up," added Vassell.

Leonard Hamilton, with over 500 wins, finally got his national championship. He has been a college head coach beginning in 1986 at Oklahoma State.

"I'm incredibly proud of this team," Hamilton stated. "From day one, they have put in the work, playing hard on both ends of the court. They all believed that this could happen, and it is truly amazing."

"This was an incredible college basketball season and both teams have a lot to be proud of," Michigan State coach Tom Izzo said.

"I cannot believe that this is the last time I am putting on my Spartan jersey," Winston said in the postgame press conference, nearly in tears. "My teammates have been so special and I will always treasure my time in East Lansing.

The game marked just the sixth time in 30 years that the championship game was decided by four points or fewer:

1994  Arkansas over Duke by 4

1999  Connecticut over Duke by 3

2003  Syracuse by Kansas by 3

2010  Duke over Butler by 2

2016  Villanova over North Carolina by 3

2020  Florida State over Michigan State by 4

The game was a nip-and tuck battle.

Florida State led 33-31 at half. Michigan State rallied to take a 47-44 lead with 13 minutes left.

M. J. Walker hit two jump shots to give the Seminoles the lead.

*M.J. Walker.*

Xavier Tillman had six points in the second half to keep Michigan State in the thick of it.

At the end, Forrest made the key free throws and Florida State won.

This was the Seminoles' second national title appearance, the first coming in 1972 (lost to UCLA).

It also marked the fifth time in six years that the national champion lost five or fewer games. Florida State finished the season at 32-5, while Michigan State completed its season at 27-10.

*Ross Obley*

# DICKIE V'S TRIVIA TEASERS

With fans having so much time during the pandemic, I figured I would throw out 50 trivia questions to test your skills. Some are easy, others challenging. Let's see how you fare…

If you go 40-50, you are awesome with a capital A, a PTP'er. If you get 30-39, you are going dancing. Make 20-29, you are a mid-major prospect. Go 10-19, work on your jump shot, baby! Good luck.

1. For the 2020-21 season, Vic Schaeffer will coach women's basketball at which school?

Mississippi State.   Texas A&M.   USC.   Texas.

2. Who won the Julius Erving Award for the 2019-20 season?

Saddiq Bey.   Luka Garza.   Obi Toppin.   Payton Pritchard.

3. Which coach has the most Final Four game wins?

Mike Krzyzewski.   John Wooden.   Adolph Rupp.   Dean Smith.

4. Which coach has the most NCAA tourney wins?

Mike Krzyzewski.   John Wooden.   Jim Boeheim.   Roy Williams.

5. Which of these men didn't take a team to the Final Four in his first season?

Larry Brown.   Denny Crum.   Bill Guthridge.   Roy Williams.

6. Which of these coaches took three different schools to the Final Four?

Hugh Durham.  Rick Pitino.  Eddie Sutton.  Lon Kruger.

7. Which of these coaches took five different teams to the NCAA Tournament?

Ben Howland.   Steve Alford.   Tubby Smith.   John Beilein.

8. Which school is currently not a member of the ACC?

Boston College.   Florida State.   Cincinnati.   Georgia Tech.

9. Who was the Most Outstanding Player in the 2003 NCAA Final Four?

Christian Laettner.   Carmelo Anthony.   Travis Ford.   Gerry McNamara.

10. Which player was the high scorer in the 1990 NCAA men's basketball championship game?

Larry Johnson.   Christian Laettner.   Anderson Hunt.   Greg Anthony.

11. Which of the following schools is not a current member of the SEC?

Florida.   Mississippi State.   Missouri.   Memphis.

12. Who was the Most Outstanding Player in the 1991 NCAA men's Final Four?

Bobby Hurley.   Christian Laettner.   Grant Hill.   Thomas Hill.

13. Which of the following Kentucky players was not a first-round NBA Draft pick?

Karl-Anthony Towns.   Willie Cayley-Stein.   Trey Lyles.   Dakari Johnson.

14. This former Arkansas Razorback led the NBA in steals during the 1986 and '87 seasons?

Sidney Moncrief.   Darrell Walker.   Scotty Thurman.   Alvin Robertson.

15. Which player on the 2019 Virginia basketball team was a nephew of Ralph Sampson?

Kihei Clark.   Braxton Key.   Casey Morsell.   Jack Sampson.

16. Which of these schools did not have Mark Turgeon as a head coach?

Wichita State.   Kansas.   Texas A&M.   Maryland.

17. He succeeded the legendary John Wooden as coach of the UCLA basketball team following the 1975 season?

Steve Lavin.   Gary Cunningham.   Gene Bartow.   Denny Crum.

18. In 1986, Cleveland State stunned this Big Ten school in the NCAA men's basketball tournament?

Ohio State.  Michigan.  Michigan State.  Indiana.

19. Who is the current head basketball coach at UCLA?

Andy Enfield.  Steve Alford.  Mick Cronin.  Steve Lavin.

20. Which two teams played in the last NCAA men's basketball championship game decided by two points?

Kansas/Syracuse.  Duke/Butler.  Connecticut/Duke.  Villanova/North Carolina.

21. Who was the Most Outstanding Player in the 1992 NCAA men's basketball tournament?

Christian Laettner.  Bobby Hurley.  Grant Hill.  Johnny Dawkins.

22. Which of the following colleges doesn't have a sports team nicknamed Tigers?

Auburn.  Texas.  Clemson.  Princeton.

23. Which of the following college stars was not picked in the 1982 NBA Draft?

James Worthy.  Ralph Sampson.  Dominique Wilkins.  Terry Cummings.

24. Which school won the 2019-20 ACC basketball regular season title?

Duke.  Virginia.  Florida State.  Louisville.

25. Which school led the nation in scoring during the 2019-20 men's college basketball regular season?

Duke.  Gonzaga.  Alabama.  NC State.

26. Bob Cousy attended which college?

Boston College.  Holy Cross.  DePaul.  Notre Dame.

27. What is the nickname of DePaul men's basketball players?

Eagles.  Hawks.  Red Warriors.  Blue Demons.

28. Which current Ivy League school was in the first NCAA Tournament in 1939?

Harvard.  Yale.  Columbia.  Brown.

29. Which college did Darrell Griffith attend?

Kentucky.  Louisville.  Notre Dame.  West Virginia.

30. Which school won back-to-back championships in the 1950's?

Ohio State.  San Francisco.  Kentucky.  Kansas.

31. Who won the first national championship in 1939?

Wyoming.  Ohio State.  Indiana.  Oregon.

32. Which college did Adrian Dantley attend?

Virginia.  Notre Dame.  Maryland.  UCLA.

33. Which of the following teams did not lose to UCLA in a championship game in the 1970's?

Memphis.  Duke.  Jacksonville.  Florida State.

34. Connecticut will be a member of which conference for the 2020-21 season?

AAC.  Big East.  Patriot.  Big Ten.

35. In 1974, NC State beat which team in the finals to win the championship?

UCLA.  Kentucky.  Marquette.  Kansas.

36. When Michigan State won the national title in 1979, which of the following was not a member of that Final Four?

Iowa.  Indiana State.  DePaul.  Penn.

37. Which of the following schools did not win and lose a championship game in the 90's?

Duke.  Arkansas.  Kentucky.  North Carolina.

38. Which player holds the Final Four record for assists in a game?

Mark Wade.  Rumeal Robinson.  Bobby Hurley.  TJ Ford.

39. Who holds the Final Four record for points by a freshman?

Carmelo Anthony.  Magic Johnson.  Mark Aguirre.  Mike O'Koren.

40. Which of the following coaches doesn't currently work in the SEC?

Kermit Davis Jr.  Tom Crean.  Cuonzo Martin.  Leonard Hamilton.

41. Which school won the 2020 CAA tournament?

College of Charleston.  Hofstra.  Delaware.  Towson.

42. Which schools were playing in the 2020 Big East tournament quarterfinals when it was halted at halftime?

Butler/Providence.  Marquette/DePaul.  Creighton/St. John's.  Villanova/Georgetown.

43. Who led the nation in steals during the 2019-20 season?

Jacob Gilyard.  Isaiah Miller.  Kihei Clark.  Cassius Winston.

44. Who led the nation in three-point FGs made per game during the 2019-20 season?

Isaiah Joe.  Antoine Davis.  Markus Howard.  Jazz Johnson.

45. Which of the following schools did not make the 1995 Final Four?

UCLA.  Arkansas.  North Carolina.  Duke.

46. Which of the following schools did not face Florida in a championship game?

Michigan State.  Connecticut.  Ohio State.  UCLA.

47. Which of the following college coaches is a member of the 2020 Basketball Hall of Fame?

Eddie Sutton.  Bobby Huggins.  Jay Wright.  Mark Few.

48. Which team did Maryland beat in the 2002 championship game?

Kansas.  Indiana.  Memphis.  Oklahoma.

49. Who is the current head coach at Vanderbilt?

Jerry Stackhouse.  Bryce Drew.  Buzz Williams.  Kermit Davis Jr.

50. North Carolina won the 2017 championship. Which of the following were not in that Final Four?

Gonzaga.  South Carolina.  Oklahoma.  Oregon.

# ANSWERS

*Coach K.*

1. He left Mississippi State for Texas.

2. Bey of Villanova.

3. Wooden with 21.

4. Coach K has 97, Williams 2nd with 79.

5. Roy Williams.

6. Pitino took Providence, Louisville, and Kentucky.

7. Tubby took Georgia, Kentucky, Minnesota, Tulsa, and Texas Tech.

8. Cincinnati is in the AAC

9. Anthony led Syracuse over Kansas.

10. Hunt with 29 points as UNLV beat Duke by 30.

11. Memphis is in the AAC.

12. Christian Laettner.

13. Dakari Johnson.

14. Alvin Robertson.

15. Braxton Key.

16. Kansas.

17. Gene Bartow.

18. Indiana.

19. Mick Cronin.

20. Duke/Butler.

21. Bobby Hurley.

22. Texas.

23. Ralph Sampson.

24. Florida State.

*Carmelo Anthony.*

*Ralph Sampson.*

*Christian Laettner.*

25. Gonzaga at 87.4 ppg.

26. Holy Cross.

27. Blue Demons.

28. Brown, Chris Berman would be proud.

29. Louisville as a member of the Doctors of Dunk.

30. The Dons with Bill Russell won in 1955 and '56.

31. Oregon beat Ohio State, 46-33.

32. Notre Dame. He played under coach Digger Phelps.

33. Duke lost to Kentucky in 1978.

34. The Huskies are leaving the AAC to return to the Big East.

35. Marquette, 76-64.

36. Iowa made it in 1980.

37. The Tar Heels won in 1993 and did not lose.

38. Mark Wade, 18 assists for UNLV vs. Indiana, NSF, 3-28-1987

39. Mark Aguirre, 34 for DePaul vs. Penn, N3d, 3-26-1979.

40. Hamilton is at Florida State in the ACC.

41. Hofstra.

42. St. John's led Creighton at half.

43. Gilyard of Richmond averaged 3.19 per game.

44. Howard led with 4.17 per game.

45. Duke made it in 1994.

46. Connecticut.

47. Congrats to Coach Sutton.

48. The Terps beat the Hoosiers, 64-52.

49. Stackhouse took over from Drew.

50. Oklahoma was in the 2016 Final Four.

# ACKNOWLEDGEMENTS

I have been so blessed in my life, both personally and professionally. This book came about in a conversation with "Hoops" Weiss and Howie Schwab as we were discussing the emptiness of not having the NCAA championship tournament in 2020. We all agreed that it would be a great idea to put my thoughts in a book about what could have been, would have been, if the season was played out. Let's make it very clear, the NCAA did the right thing in making the decision to cancel March Madness due to the coronavirus pandemic. Absolutely, our priority must be the health and safety of everyone.

I must personally thank Hoops Weiss, Howie Schwab, and my wife and family for their contributions in helping me along the way.

*My better half for 49 years!*

*My family. My grandchildren, daughters, and their husbands. All eleven of us.*

Also, a tribute must go to my second family...all of my colleagues at ESPN who have been vital to me throughout my entire career.

*With Rece Davis, Brooke Weisbrod, and Mike Shiffman, ESPN Vice President of NBA and College Basketball Production.*

*At my 2019 Gala with Holly Rowe, winner of the John Saunders Courage Award for inspiring many in her courageous battle vs. cancer.*

*My ESPN broadcast team for the last few years: Kim Belton, producer; Bob Wischusen, play-by-play; and Kris Budden, sideline reporter.*

This book would not have happened without the super work done by Hoops Weiss, a Hall of Fame journalist, who is a guru when it comes to college sports.

I certainly can't say enough about Howie Schwab and the dedication and research he did in working on this project.

*Dick "Hoops" Weiss joins me at my 2019 Gala at the Ritz-Calrton, Sarasota.*

*Howie and Suzie Schwab, Lorraine and Dick Vitale enjoying a long lunch together.*

I would like to recognize and thank Sandy Montag, CEO of The Montag Group, and my personal representative, Susan Lipton. I have been fortunate to have been represented by Sandy (first at IMG, and now at The Montag Group) for the past 35 years. Susan has been working with me for the past two decades. They have done an amazing job for me and my career.

One of the things that excites me about this book is that every dollar that I would make will go to The V Foundation for Pediatric Cancer Research. I hope that you will join MY TEAM in helping to raise money for kids battling cancer. Simply go to DickVitale.com to DONATE. Your donation will go directly to The V Foundation. I thank you from the bottom of my heart.

- Dick Vitale

*Susan Lipton and Sandy Montag of The Montag Group, my representation for over three decades.*

I would like to thank the following people for all their assistance and support for our latest project. First, my wife Joanie, who has co-authored books with me in the past and has been a rock throughout this whole process; Dick and Lorraine Vitale, wonderful people who really care about their community and the V Foundation and their daughters Sherri and Terri; Howie Schwab, the best research guy I ever worked with, and his wife Suzie; John Feinstein, a brilliant mind who has always made basketball fun for me; Bob Ryan, the legendary columnist, and his wife Elaine; Mike Nicloy, Lyda Rose Haerle, Sara Sauer, Reji Laberje, and Griff Mill of Nico 11 Publishing and Design; Mike Flynn, the CEO of Blue Star, who has always been able to see into the future of the sport; Joe and Betty Ann Cassidy; Scott and Suzanne Schenker and their family Hayden, Madison, Delaney, Griffin, and Danielle; Jeanine Reynolds Delaney and her children Tim, Andrew, and Matt; Karl Grentz and his wife Theresa, who was the best player of her generation and belongs in the Naismith Hall of Fame; Lesley Visser; Liza Lank; Lea Miller, the driving force behind Battle4Atlantis, and her husband Jim Tooley of USA Basketball; my attorney Rick Troncelliti; John Akers of Basketball Times; Pat Plunkett and his wife Trish and children Mairead, Ailis, and Aine; Steve Richardson from the FWAA and Malcom Moran from the U.S. Basketball Writers; Jay Wright and Mike Sheridan; Dave Goren of the ASMA; Brian Morrison and John Paquette; Alan Cutler and Adam Berkowitz; Dick Jerardi; Dr. David Raezer, my favorite all-time doctor; Sam Albano; Jerry McLaughlin; Larry Pearlstein; Steve Kirchner, Mark Whicker, and Robyn Norwood; Val Ackerman, Billy Reynolds; the late, great Larry Donald; Danny Gavitt, and David Worlock from the NCAA; Sean Ford and Craig Miller from USA Basketball; all the folks in the Big 5; Sadie and the late Charlie; the Guys, and all the coaches and players in college basketball who have made coverage of the sport so much fun for me over the years. Some of the background and statistics were put together with the help of previous books I did with Dick Vitale over the past 32 years. Thanks.

- Dick Weiss

I was watching the Big East tournament game between Creighton and St. John's when the college basketball season collapsed.

At least my alma mater led at the final halftime of the campaign.

I spoke to Dick Vitale, Dick Weiss, and Mike Nicloy about this book project. It became a reality, written in little more than a month. We all felt it would be special for the fans.

This effort came at the right time as it served as a distraction from the nightmare plaguing our nation. Being sheltered in my condo for so long actually became a labor of love besides a necessity. College basketball has meant so much to me for over 40 years.

It was an honor to work with Dick and Lorraine Vitale, Dick Weiss and his wife Joanie, Mike Nicloy, and Reji Laberge.

Special thanks to the Sports Information Directors who were so wonderful answering our requests.

America should always thank the doctors, nurses, social workers, and food service personnel during trying times.

I hope you enjoy reading about *The Lost Season*. It was emotional for all of us.


- Howie Schwab

# ABOUT THE AUTHORS

**D**ick Vitale is college basketball's top analyst and ambassador. His thorough knowledge of the game is brought forth in an enthusiastic, passionate, sometimes controversial—but never boring—style.

In 2018, Vitale began his fortieth season at ESPN. He joined the worldwide leader in sports during the 1979-80 season, just after the network's September 1979 launch, when he called the network's first-ever major NCAA basketball game, Wisconsin at DePaul, on Dec. 5, 1979. Since then, he's called over one thousand games.

Vitale has authored thirteen books, including *Dick Vitale's Mount Rushmores of College Basketball – Solid Gold Prime Time Performers From My Four Decades at ESPN*, *It's Awesome, Baby! 75 Years of Memories and a Lifetime of Opinions on the Game I Love*, *Dick Vitale's Living a Dream*, all co-authored with Dick Weiss; *Getting a W in the Game of Life*, co-authored with Reji Laberje; and children's book, *Dickie V's ABCs and 1-2-3s*.

### Hall of Fame Career

In 2008, Vitale received the sport's ultimate honor when he was selected as an inductee into the Naismith Memorial Basketball Hall of Fame.

Vitale has been selected for a total of fourteen halls of fame: National Italian American Sports Hall of Fame, the Elmwood Park, N.J., Hall of Fame (his hometown), the Sarasota Boys and Girls Club Hall of Fame (inducted in inaugural class of 2001), the Five-Star Basketball Camp Hall of Fame (2003), the University of Detroit Hall of Fame, the Florida Sports Hall of Fame in 1996 (he's a resident of the state), the East Rutherford, N.J., Hall of Fame (1985), the National Collegiate Basketball Hall of Fame (2008), the Naismith Memorial Basketball Hall of Fame (2008), Sarasota Community Archives Hall of Fame (2009), the Little League Museum Hall of Excellence (2012), the National Sportscasters

*Susan Lipton, rep for The Montag Group.; Dick Vitale, Sandy Montag, CEO of The Montag Group; and Bob Costas at the National Sports Broadcasting Hall of Fame induction ceremony.*

and Sportswriters Association Awards (NSSA) Hall of Fame (2013), Wooden Cup Award (2017), and the National Sports Broadcasting Hall of Fame (2018).

A few of Vitale's recent prestigious honors: In 2000, Vitale was recognized with the NABC Cliff Wells Appreciation Award for outstanding service to the college basketball coaching community and college basketball in general, and in 2001, the College Sports Information Directors of America (CoSIDA) presented him with the Jake Wade Award for contributions to college athletics, and in 2008, CoSIDA honored Vitale with the prestigious Keith Jackson Eternal Flame Award given to an individual who, or an organization which, has made a lasting contribution to intercollegiate athletics, has demonstrated a long and consistent commitment to excellence, and has been a loyal supporter of CoSIDA and its mission. Additionally, as part of the Washington Speakers Bureau, he has spoken at many corporate events about his efforts as a broadcaster and philanthropist. In 2002, the Florida Association of Community Corrections presented him with their President's Humanitarian Award for his work with young people; while in 2003, Vitale was honored with the first-ever Ethics and Sportsmanship in Sports Media Award given by the Institute for International Sport, as well as the National Pathfinder Award, co-presented by Indiana Sports Corporation and Indiana Black Expo to individuals who have demonstrated a dedicated commitment to improving the lives of America's youth. In 2008, he was selected as the recipient of the 2008 Naismith Men's Outstanding Contributor to Basketball (pays tribute to individuals who made a significant impact on college basketball). The Tampa Bay Sports Commission awarded Vitale with their Lee Roy Selmon Lifetime Achievement Award in 2011 for his incredible support in the Tampa Bay sports community. In 2012, the *Tampa Bay Business Journal* honored Vitale as Philanthropist of the Year during their annual Health Care Heroes event. In the same year, Vitale was also named one of 13 Magnetic Men by PARC, a non-profit organization whose mission is to provide opportunities for children and adults with developmental disabilities. In addition to being inducted into their hall of fame in 2013, the National Sportscasters and Sportswriters Association named Vitale the Sportscaster of the Year. In 2014, he earned several awards, including the Vincent T. Lombardi Memorial Award, presented by UNICO, the Man of the Year Award from the American Cancer Society, and the Humanitarian of the Year from his alma mater Seton Hall University. The AutoZone Liberty Bowl recognized Vitale with the Distinguished Citizen Award in 2015 for his work raising money for cancer research. Vitale was also recognized by the National Association of Basketball Coaches with the Man of the Year Award. In 2019, he was recognized with the Sports Emmys' Lifetime Achievement Award. Vitale received the 2020 NCAA President's Gerald R. Ford Award, which recognizes an individual who has provided significant leadership as an advocate for college sports.

He continues to participate on selection committees for both the Naismith and Wooden Awards and is a member of The Associated Press voting panel for the Top 25. He is also a voter for the Hall of Fame's Bob Cousy Awards.

Vitale graduated from Seton Hall University with a Bachelor of Science Degree in Business Administration. He also earned a Master's Degree in education from William Paterson College, and has 32 graduate credits beyond the Master's Degree in Administration.

Vitale's roots are in teaching the game he's loved since a child. Following graduation from college, he got a job teaching at Mark Twain Elementary School in Garfield, N.J., where he also coached junior high school football and basketball. He began coaching at the high school level at Garfield High School, where he coached for one season (1963-64). He then earned four state sectional championships, two consecutive state championships, and 35 consecutive victories during his seven years at his alma mater, East Rutherford, New Jersey, High School (1964-70).

He joined Rutgers University for two years (1970-72) as an assistant coach, helping to recruit Phil Sellers and Mike Dabney, two cornerstones on an eventual NCAA Final Four team (1976).

Vitale then coached at the University of Detroit (1973-77), compiling a winning percentage of .722 (78-30), which included a 21-game winning streak during the 1976-77 season when the team participated in the NCAA Tournament. Included in the streak was a victory in Milwaukee over Al McGuire's eventual national champion Marquette team. In April 1977, Vitale was named Athletic Director at the University of Detroit and later that year was named the United Fund's Detroit Man of the Year. In May 1978, he was named head coach of the NBA's Detroit Pistons, which he coached during the 1978-79 season, prior to joining ESPN.

*Dick Vitale Courts at Clinton Playground in East Rutherford, New Jersey, where Vitale coached high school athletics.*

### *Philanthropy*

Vitale is on the Board of Directors of The V Foundation, a non-profit organization dedicated to finding a cure for cancer and founded in 1993 by ESPN and the late Jim Valvano (an organization with has since raised over $200 million for cancer research). He hosts the annual "Dick Vitale Gala" in Florida benefiting the V Foundation, which has raised more than $30 million to date, gathering numerous celebrities to raise money and honor individuals such as Mike Krzyzewski, Bob Knight, Pat Summitt, Billy Donovan, Tom Izzo, Jay Wright, and Nick Saban, and Robin Roberts.

For many years he's awarded five scholarships annually to the Boys & Girls Club of Sarasota, Florida. His involvement with the organization was highlighted in April 1999 with the "Dick Vitale Sports Night," an annual banquet that has raised more than $1 million. In April 2000, in recognition of Vitale's support for the Boys and Girls Club, it was announced that a new building would be named The Dick Vitale Physical Education and Health Training Center. A statue of him stands in front of the Training Center. Vitale was inducted into the Sarasota's Boys and Girls Club Hall of Fame at the 2001 Dinner. In 2002, Sarasota magazine named him one of the area's most influential citizens.

Dick Vitale was born in Passaic, New Jersey, and resided in his youth in Garfield and Elmwood Park, New Jersey. He and his wife Lorraine now reside in Lakewood Ranch, Florida (Sarasota-Bradenton area), and have two daughters, Terri and Sherri, who both attended Notre Dame on tennis scholarships, and who both graduated with MBAs from the Golden Dome. Terri and her husband Chris have two children, Sydney, 18, who is starting her diaper dandy year at the University of Notre Dame, where she will be a member of the Irish tennis team; and Ryan, 16, who is currently at the prestigious IMG Academy in Bradenton, Florida, where he competes on their varsity and national lacross teams, and he is a rising junior. Sherri and her husband Thomas have three children; twins Jake and Connor, 17, rising Seniors and blue chip national junior tennis players who have committed to Duke University; and Ava, 14, a rising freshman who, like her brothers, is a highly rated junior and noational tennis player.

The Vitale's proud involvement with Notre Dame includes the endowment of the Dick Vitale Family Scholarship, presented annually to Irish undergraduates who participate in Notre Dame Sports and activities that do not provide financial aid. Recipients over the years have included the school's Leprechaun mascot, cheerleaders, and band members.

*The family at Dickie V's 80th birthday bash.*

Dick is a popular figure even outside of sports television. He's made cameo appearances in several movies such as *The Naked Gun, Hoop Dreams, Blue Chips, The Sixth Man, He Got Game, Love and Basketball,* and *Jury Duty.*

**Dick Weiss** is a Hall of Fame sports columnist who worked for more than 40 years with the *Philadelphia Daily News*, the *New York Daily News*, and currently works for Blue Star Media, covering college, NBA, and international basketball. He has covered 47 NCAA Final Fours and 35 national championship games in college football and was inducted into the national Sportswriters Hall of Fame. Weiss is the past president of the Football Writers of America and the U.S. Basketball Writers Association and was the youngest recipient of the prestigious Curt Gowdy Award for media excellence from the Naismith Hall of Fame and the Bert McGraine Award from the FWAA and the College Football Hall of Fame, the highest honor given to a college football writer. He is also a member of the U.S. Basketball Writers Hall of Fame, the Philadelphia Big 5 Hall of Fame, the Philadelphia Sports Hall of Fame, and the Journalism Hall of Fame award from his alma mater, Temple.

He was inducted into the Pennsylvania Sports Hall of Fame in 2019 and received a second media award from the Big East Conference in 2020. This is his 14th book. He has co-authored 13 books with Hall of Famers Rick Pitino, John Calipari, Dick Vitale, and Theresa Grentz, two of them with his wife Joan, an award winning editor. The couple resides in Havertown, Pennsylvania.

**Howie Schwab** began his career of covering college athletics back in 1980 at *College and Pro Football Newsweekly*. He worked at ESPN for 26 years and enjoyed stints at Sports Jeopardy and Fox Sports, where he most recently served as the network's college basketball bracketologist. He is currently involved with Cameo, Starsona, and Clickstream.

Howie and his wife, Suzie, reside in Fort Lauderdale, Florida.